THIS CREW OF MINE

THIS
CREW
OF
MINE

GETTING OUT OF ORGANIZED CRIME ALIVE

TROY SKINNER

Windows
of Vision

Omaha, NE

Windows of Vision Books
c/o Concierge Marketing Publishing Services
13518 L. Street
Omaha, NE 68137

Paperback ISBN: 978-0-9894729-1-3
Kindle ISBN: 978-0-9894729-2-0
LCCN: 2013940698

Library of Congress Cataloging information on file with publisher.

Design and production: Concierge Marketing, Inc.
Printed in the United States of America.
10 9 8 7 6 5 4 3 2

CONTENTS

CHAPTER ONE

ABNORMALLY YOUNG

Let me begin by saying living a life of crime is not glamorous. A life of crime can bring power and a lot of money, but it also has consequences. I know firsthand because I lived that life. I was a gangster, a thug, and a criminal. My name is Troy Skinner.

I was born in Fremont, Nebraska, on April 11, 1969. I was the second son born to Thomas, a laborer, and Donna Skinner, a housewife. My brother, Rowdy, was just three years older than me.

Right after my birth, all four of us moved to Lake Minatare, Nebraska. Minatare was a small town. There were maybe a total of 300 people in the whole town. Our family lived on the lake so Rowdy and I kept ourselves entertained by fishing and swimming when we weren't attending school.

At the age of ten, my childhood was about to change. The year was 1979. This was the year I would begin to learn what loyalty and friendship was all about. My brother was hanging around a kid by the name of Billy, who was three years older

1

than my brother. Billy lived about four miles from us on another lake called Lake Alice. Billy showed up at our house one Saturday morning really upset and asked my brother if he could speak to my mom and dad.

Rowdy let Billy in the house, my dad asked him to sit at the kitchen table and Billy began telling us that his mom and dad had kicked him out of the house, and that he needed a place to stay. Dad was reluctant at first and told him there would be rules. For example, 9:00 p.m. curfew, no drinking, no smoking cigarettes in or near the house, no drug use, and he had to help out with the chores of the farm. It seems odd now to think there were rules about smoking and drinking, but those things were going on even at that age.

For about the first three weeks everything was going well, until one Friday afternoon when a black four-door sedan pulled into the driveway. Billy and Rowdy went outside to Billy's car and grabbed a brown paper bag and gave it to the driver of the black sedan. I had asked Rowdy what that was all about and what was in the bag. Rowdy told me that it was marijuana and to keep my mouth shut and gave me a ten dollar bill. To a ten-year-old kid back in 1979, that was a lot of money.

When we went back into the house, dad and mom were standing in the living room. My dad asked us what was going on. I put my head down and did not want to answer, nor did Rowdy or Billy. Dad took us outside and over to the side of the house. He told Billy he should pack his things and had to leave within the hour, and as for Rowdy and I, we were grounded for the rest of the summer.

My dad got a better paying job about six months later, so we moved from the Lake to another small town about thirteen miles away called Bayard, Nebraska, that was highly populated with Mexicans. Right from the start as Caucasians, we were seen as outsiders.

It was here in Bayard at a softball game that Rowdy and I would meet four Mexican brothers: Jose, Santiago, Carlos, and Roberto. Jose was the oldest and the strongest. He made it known he was the leader in his family. This was because his father had passed away several years earlier.

Santiago was the second oldest. He was the weakest link in the family. Getting into trouble was not something he enjoyed, but he was dedicated to his brother, Jose, as we all were. He was the oldest and knew how to use martial arts to win a fight. In a split second, Jose would have our back in any situation, and it made us feel safe.

Carlos was my age and would become the closest to me. Roberto was the youngest but at the age of eight, he stood his ground and didn't back down from anything. The Garcia brothers, Rowdy and I would become instant friends. We began hanging out every day and staying out late. The six of us became inseparable.

It was June and there were a couple of months left before school would begin. The Garcia brothers had quite a reputation. They were known around town as thugs. You see, the Garcia brothers drank, did drugs, and beat down anyone who crossed them. Knowing I was protected by the brothers was a damn good feeling. I could do and say whatever I wanted and knew they had my back as well as my brother's.

The first time I was really made aware of their reputation was when I was getting picked on by a boy named Kenny. Somehow, I would always run into Kenny. He was much bigger than me. Kenny would constantly push me around or make fun of me. One day I mentioned this to Santiago and Jose, and Jose told me "We'll take care of it." One afternoon, the Garcia brothers and I walked to Kenny's house and right there in his front yard, we surrounded him.

Jose was the only one who spoke; and as he spoke, he slapped Kenny hard in the face to make sure he had his undivided attention. "You fuck with Troy, then you fuck with us. And when you fuck with us you will get hurt." That's all that was said, but I felt vindicated and I thought, "Wow, these guys really do have our backs and this is the way to take care of problems."

Kenny went running inside his house without looking back. From that day on, I was loyal to the Garcia brothers. I had to be loyal because in my mind I now owed them. I had witnessed firsthand the impact they had on others, and I craved the same kind of respect and loyalty from other people as well.

◆　　◆　　◆

The rest of the summer, I was gaining respect and loyalty from others because the word had gotten around about our message to Kenny. To keep from getting bored, Rowdy, myself and the Garcia brothers started hanging out at Rubes tavern. This was the local bar in town and this was back when it wasn't a big deal for minors to be in a bar and play pool without their parents. It was there where I had my first run-in with the cops. My Uncle Art was a regular at the bar. He stood about six feet tall and weighed 180 pounds. He wasn't a real big man but he made himself known wherever he went.

My Uncle Art loved to play pool and he loved to gamble. If someone tried to get out of paying their dues, Uncle Art would take other means to get his money.

I remember one night in the bar, Uncle Art was getting into an argument with a man about some money the man owed my uncle over a poker game. They both walked through the bar and outside where they continued arguing. Just as my brother, the Garcia brothers and I got outside, we saw our uncle hit the ground. He was knocked out cold. Jose ran back inside and came back out with an empty beer bottle, and in his best Billy Jack one-liner told the man, "I'm gonna take my right foot and put it up the left side of your face, and there's not a damn thing you can do about it." Jose was smaller than the man, so the kick didn't have much of an effect on him. The man shook it off and lunged, and then Jose smashed the guy over the head with the bottle as he went to the ground like a sack of potatoes. We were all laughing because we were kids and we knew the line was from a movie and we had just seen Jose kick a much bigger guy's ass.

In a couple of minutes, the town's only patrol car was pulling up to the scene. That was time for us to take off and run to the local park and hide out for a while. On the way, Rowdy slipped and fell, sliding along the concrete and gravel about ten feet. Out of breath when we reached the park, we looked at one another and started laughing and making remarks about Rowdy's hands and knees which were all bloody and caked with gravel, and the guy's head that Jose had split open.

What we had just done was leave another message to everyone in town. No one should fuck with the Skinner family or the Garcia family. This was a bond, even as a preteen, I believed would never end and could never be broken.

— CHAPTER TWO —

LEARNING FAST

It didn't take long for word to spread through town as to what happened. My Uncle Art was back at the bar within a few days, and we never saw the other guy again. We heard rumors that he wasn't from Bayard and that he had left town. So much for my uncle getting his money, I guess.

◆　　◆　　◆

It was the end of August and Rowdy and I were back in school. I was now in the sixth grade and Rowdy was in the ninth grade. The Garcia brothers attended school on occasion, and they smoked and dealt small amounts of marijuana not only in town, but in school as well.

My cousin Teresa went to school with my brother. She had met the Garcia brothers and partied with us a couple of times over the summer. Jose was already in trouble at school and had asked Teresa to hide a joint in her locker. Unfortunately, another classmate had heard about the joint and reported to the Principal. Before the school day ended, my cousin's locker had been searched and Rowdy and Teresa were sitting in Principal Miller's office. Nothing needed to be said, they knew what they were there for. With the threat of being kicked out of school and having to face our parents, Rowdy and Teresa told Mr. Miller that the joint belonged to Jose. The Principal saw this as an opportunity to kick the Garcia brothers out of school, so he suspended Santiago and Jose for three days and the police were called to question both of them about the joint. The police finally had a reason to charge them with possession because they, and everyone else in town, knew the Garcias were dealing drugs.

◆   ◆   ◆

Rowdy, Teresa, and I knew that the Garcia brothers would want revenge for this, and so basically all three of us imprisoned ourselves in our homes after school, only venturing out when necessary. A couple of weeks passed, and we heard nothing until one Tuesday afternoon when the Garcia brothers pulled up to our house in a van. My mother met them at the door and we heard her say in a stern voice, "Rowdy and Troy are not allowed to hang out with you boys anymore." Then she slammed the door in their face. The next day a good friend of the family came over to inform my mother that the Garcia brothers were making serious threats on the whole family. There were threats made on the family cars and house, and the friend also heard that the Garcia brothers were plotting to take Rowdy and I out to the country, and we "probably would not be coming back."

So much for that bond that I thought would never be broken. This was my first awakening that the severity of a bond could be dangerous and even deadly when broken.

◆　　◆　　◆

Within about a week after hearing threats all over town, my mother thought it was best if we packed up and moved. My mother wanted to be closer to her side of the family anyway, which was in Fremont, Nebraska. So we moved into a house on the south side of Fremont. Mom and Dad were not happy about having to start all over again, but I would embark on a new journey.

— CHAPTER THREE —

MOVING TO A NEW PLACE

The first week of my new school in my new town was okay. By the very first Friday, I was hanging out with who I thought was the best looking girl in school. Her name was Kari. She had dark brown eyes and long hair. During recess, we sat on the grass next to the concrete playground. While other boys and girls were swinging and playing hopscotch, Kari and I would sit and she would fill me in on all the other students and what she thought of them. I was all ears as we also flirted back and forth with each other, as much as sixth graders do.

The popular guys in school became jealous that she was choosing to spend more time with me over them, and on several occasions they told me to leave her alone. But I didn't listen. Nope. Nobody was going to tell me I couldn't hang out with her, plus she was too good-looking and too nice not to hang out with.

I walked home with Kari every day. A few weeks passed, and on a sunny Thursday after school I was walking home with Kari as usual, and three of our classmates came up behind us. They proceeded to make fun of us and started pushing Kari. They knew that would piss me off, and before I knew it my right fist connected to the face of Joe. Joe fell to the ground, and as I turned to kick him, the other two grabbed me from behind and knocked me down. Then all three of them started kicking me in my head. As they kicked, they cursed, "Douche bag! Leave her alone. We warned you!" I heard Kari yelling "Stop! Please stop!" After a couple more kicks, they stopped and took off and I got up and ran home, ashamed and embarrassed, leaving Kari standing there in shock to walk home on her own.

On my way home that day, I passed a boy practicing with a pair of nunchucks. I watched in amazement how quickly and smoothly he swung the two pieces of wood attached by a chain the middle above his head, between his legs, under his arms, behind his back. I was in awe. He saw me watching him. I was cut up and bleeding, and he stopped and approached me to ask, "What the hell happened to you?" I told him the whole story. He gave me his pair of nunchucks and said, "Keep these, and carry them with you wherever you go." I shook his hand and said "Thanks man. What's your name?" He replied, "Dave. I live right over there." He pointed to a house three doors from mine. Dave was a grade higher than me, but from then on we were a team.

The next morning came, and I did not want to go to school. I slipped out of bed and grabbed the nunchucks that I had hidden under my bed. They would be coming to school with me. I put on a light jacket and dropped the nunchucks down my jacket sleeve. I didn't take my jacket off all day. Nobody was going to jump me again.

School let out as usual. I met Kari at our usual place. This was it, I was ready this time. Out of the corner of my eye I could see the boys heading my way but I kept walking with Kari by my side. *Not this time,* I thought to myself.

We made it to the other side of the school grounds just as the boys caught up to us. I pulled the nunchucks from my sleeve and popped Joe on the top of the head before he and his two friends could use my head as a soccer ball again. Joe fell to the ground screaming. The other two ran back inside the school to get the principal. Kari looked at me and smiled. "They deserved it," she said. Little did I know at the time, I could have killed him with those nunchucks. Luckily, that didn't happen, but it did solidify my position on the playground.

Principal Williams suddenly appeared out of nowhere, grabbed me from behind and ordered me back into the school. I told him right away Kari had nothing to do with it. Mr. Williams called my parents to the school, and I was given my first suspension. No school for me on Monday and I wasn't to return until Wednesday. The look on my mother's face made me wish I was at school. Joe did not get suspended because the principal said, "He has been through enough." The principal never knew those three boys had been bullying me and had beaten me up the day prior.

What happened spread through the neighborhood like a virus. My name was becoming known very quickly. Saturday afternoon I was outside and several of the neighborhood kids came up to talk to me. I was making friends. When I went back to school on Wednesday everyone knew my name—or so it seemed—because none of the students were making fun of me or talking behind my back, but instead now wanted to be my friend. I had the power and fear from kids in school, which made me feel important and respected—a feeling I had been seeking for myself since the day I watched Jose bust the man in the head at the bar months earlier.

I still walked home with Kari, not to mention several other girls and a few boys. The last few months of school flew by because I was no longer afraid, and I was spending time with all the kids that now wanted to be my friends.

Junior high was just weeks away. Another new school where my name was not known and a whole bunch of new kids I had to get to know too. So I spent my summer hanging out with the neighborhood kids to make sure I didn't fall out of popularity. I also made friends with kids that were already in junior high so I would know some kids from day one.

Throughout the summer, my new group of friends and I hung out a lot at my friend Tim's house. He lived just three blocks down the street from me. I started hanging out late every night drinking. Older girls would come over often and we would sit around and drink.

Tim's mother, was hardly ever home so we could drink all we wanted at his place because his mother always kept a stocked bar. She worked at a bar and closed every night. We never got caught drinking her liquor because we would simply drink a little from each bottle and then fill it back up with water.

If we got bored we walked the streets, and if any other kids bothered us we would often fight our way out of the situation and go on about our business. The summer between sixth and seventh grades seemed like a violent one, given our ages; but in hindsight, it was shockingly violent for kids that were not even in junior high yet. It only got worse from there.

CHAPTER FOUR

STARTING JUNIOR AND SENIOR HIGH

Before we knew it, that summer had come to an end. Junior high had finally come. I believed Junior high was going to be hard, but it was actually pretty easy for me. Not the schoolwork, mind you, but dealing with the kids. I had built a strategy in my head that summer before of how to get things done, who to trust, and and how to get by. Throughout my seventh and eighth grade years I got into a lot of pushing and shoving, but only two major fights with other kids.

Ninth grade was a different story. I started staying out later, drinking more and going to all the parties I could. I liked being with the hoodlum crowd because they were considered bad ass and powerful. I felt comfortable with them.

Dave and I were wasting time one Saturday afternoon by riding around on his motorcycle waiting for a Nebraska Football game party to begin. At about 5:30 we were on our way to the party when a cop pulled behind us. We took off because Dave did not have a motorcycle license. We lost the cop. Knowing the cop would be searching the area, we hid the motorcycle in the backyard of the party we attended.

Walking into the party we told people what had just happened and immediately we were the life of the party. Several hours passed and the party was growing bigger by the minute. Sometime between 11:00 p.m. and midnight, five police officers knocked at the door. Everyone at the party started panicking and hiding their marijuana and beer cans. One of the officers on the scene walked out the back door of the house to see if anybody was out back—it was the same officer who had chased Dave and I earlier in the evening. He came back in the house and looked at each one of us. He pointed to the back yard and said in deep, loud voice, "Who owns the bike in the back yard?" There was a dead silence as he looked into the eyes of everyone in the room. No one answered, so he and his fellow officers took a defensive stance and the first officer said "If no one wants to fess up to it, we'll just take all of you to jail for MIP." After a momentary silence, the officer said "Alright then, let's go. We're taking everyone to jail." Suddenly, a voice from the crowd said "It's Dave's," as several other kids pointed to Dave. Two officers grabbed Dave and started walking him out. He remained completely silent and in shock that his friends had ratted him out.

Suddenly I felt guilty that Dave might be going to jail alone, so I confessed to being with him during the chase. Two officers took us outside and put us in the back of a squad car as the cops dispersed the party and told everyone to go home, which they did very quickly.

Sitting in the squad car, the idea of jail whirled around in my head. The officer finally got into the car with us. For what seemed like an hour, he chewed our asses and scared the hell out of us. He then drove us to our houses. I remember seeing my mother and my Uncle Kenny as we pulled up to my house. I didn't want to get out of the car; I knew my ass was grass. As I got out of the car I looked to the ground. I couldn't look my mother or my Uncle in the eyes. The look of anger and disappointment on their faces made me feel ashamed. I had let my mother down once more.

◆　　　◆　　　◆

The end of the ninth grade had finally arrived. However, I got one hell of a blow from the school. I was being held back because of my chronic tardiness and no-care attitude. I had flunked the majority of my classes.

I had a lot of time on my hands over the summer, and developed a fascination with organized crime. I watched movies and read every book, magazine and newspaper article I could get my hands on to educate myself about the Mafia, Organized Crime, and the Mob. I became very familiar with Al Capone and how he ruled Chicago and the bootleg booze empire. I studied the operations of the five major crime families, including John Gotti and the Gambino family.

I fantasized about starting my own little crew. I had already established fear in kids in school and the neighborhood, now I needed the money. What I needed were five or six loyal friends. I needed loyalty from those who would not rat each other out. I ended up finding four good friends that I could trust.

We went to parties and started stealing cassette tapes, money, jackets, and painkillers out of the host's medicine cabinets. Anything we could steal, we would claim as ours. If we weren't invited to a party and happened to hear about it, we would show up anyway. People knew they would have to deal with all five of us at once, so nobody asked us to leave.

After a few months, we started bringing in the cash by selling the things we stole to other kids. Then we started dressing a little better and money was always in our pockets.

Soon, we became obsessed with the idea of having even more cash, so we started buying small amounts of marijuana and white crosses from dealers that we knew from hanging out with other hoodlums. We bought the drugs with the intent on selling them and making more money. By this time, the crew had grown to nine or ten guys.

I started having a lot of parties myself, and was quickly introduced to cocaine. More money was coming in but unfortunately, at the same time, I started using the drugs myself. My reputation for selling drugs and being a bad ass had grown to such a height that anywhere I went people knew my name or at least knew of me in Fremont. It was at this time, I started realizing the profit potential of bringing the hoods, jocks and preps together at parties to get along— at least at the parties on weekends. Come Monday each week at school, we resumed our roles as arch rivals.

As I became more "business minded," my schoolwork went downhill. I was either too hung over, too tired, or too strung out to go to school, so I ended up quitting. With the money I was making I joined Izaak Walton, a membership-only conservation organization right on the outside of Fremont that had three lakes and two cabins on it.

I needed a bigger place for my parties and Izaak Walton was the perfect place— or so I thought.

All the parties were going great in the beginning, until I decided to have one of the biggest parties I had ever had. I printed up flyers and put them on the windshields of cars at the high school starting on a Monday, and returned every day before and after school handing out flyers.

Friday afternoon came, and I got my Uncle Kenny to buy me three sixteen-gallon kegs. I went out to the cabin at Izaak Walton around 6:00 p.m. and started setting up. I had also brought along a shotgun that was given to me as a gift. I sawed the barrel off making it only seventeen inches in length and engraved my name on it. I brought the gun in case anybody got too out of control. I knew there would be hoods, jocks, preps, and others from the school. I started a fire in the fireplace and proceeded to hook up my stereo.

People started to show up around 9:00 p.m.. The cabin was full and people were already standing outside in a line waiting to get to the kegs. My pockets were filled with the $5.00 bills that I was charging for a cover at the door.

I was sitting on a picnic table just inside the entrance by the kegs. I had the cups and a black magic marker with me. As a party guest arrived, they paid me $5, I gave them a cup, and I marked their hand to show they had paid to get in. The kegs were to the left at the end of the table I was sitting on, so a person had to go through me to get into the party. I ran the whole operation, and Rowdy helped out with security (while he was partying). The gun was behind me and two of the best looking preppy girls in the entire school had their arms around me the whole night. A hoodlum with a preppy girl on each arm? Unheard of! But that was what I was trying to accomplish with this party.

Looking around the room I saw everybody getting along like friends. The stuck up kids and the hoods partying together! Just like *Breakfast Club*. That was a good feeling and was turning out to be profitable. I envisioned having a party like this every Friday night. The money, the girls, the booze.

The party grew even bigger, and by 11:00 p.m. those arriving later started parking their cars out on the side of the highway right outside of Izaak Walton and walking up to the cabin.

I remember leaning over to give one of the girls that had her arm around me a kiss and just then I heard someone yell "Cops!" It was too late. The cops were in the door. Everyone froze.

One of the officers yelled, "Who is responsible for this party?" He looked right at me; I recognized him.

I responded by saying, "You couldn't have picked a worse fucking time. This is my party. I thought this was private property and cops couldn't come out here."

The officer replied, "We can when the chairmen and other members of Izaak Walton ask us to." He continued on, "We are going to let everybody go home. Troy, you are going to jail for MIP, selling liquor without a license and contributing to the delinquency of minors."

Everybody left. My brother and a friend stayed behind to see what was going to happen to me. The officers made me clean up the cabin and made my brother and I carry the kegs to the back of one of the squad cars. As we were lifting the last keg into the trunk, I dropped my end and it hit the tail light and broke it. I started laughing. The officer didn't find it amusing, but I knew there was nothing he could do about it because he was the one who made us put it in the trunk.

One of the other officers followed me back to the cabin to have me shut off the lights and lock the door. I got nervous, as I knew the shotgun was still in there. When the police first came in I had quickly slid it under the table. I tried to shut off the lights as fast as I could, but the officer got a glimpse of the gun. He walked in and picked it up.

"Is this yours?" He asked.

"I don't know who brought that," I replied.

"Why is your name engraved on it then?"

"Well then it must be mine. You caught me, Sherlock."

He put me in handcuffs right away and I was off to jail. When I arrived at the jail, the officer started finger printing me and booking me in as an inmate, one of the guards told me my bond would be 10 percent of $1000. I used some of the money I had made from the party to bond out because the officer had not confiscated the money. Fremont police had become famous for making mistakes or somehow not completing their jobs.

I had requested a public defender for the first time I appeared in court. The day of sentencing my attorney was able to get all the charges dropped except the MIP charge. I got one year probation, and in addition, I was ordered to attend an outpatient treatment program. I had to attend AA meetings twice a week, and had to complete sixty community service hours. So that year, I was pretty quiet in town, except for my occasional appearances at a close friend's house to have a few drinks. The whole year, I worked odd jobs here and there, lived at my mother's house, and concentrated on completing my probation successfully so that I would not end up in jail.

— CHAPTER FIVE —

LETTING THE HEAT COOL DOWN

———

After my probation was over, I decided I would let things cool down in Fremont for a while. I had heard about a dance place in Omaha, Nebraska, on the radio called Sprite Night. So on weekends, I joined my brother and five of our friends at Sprite Night and a place called Buffalo Bills. These were the hot teen dance places in Omaha at the time.

Rowdy was 21 and I was 18. We went every weekend with the same group of friends. Rowdy bought the alcohol and we sat out in the parking lot and drank awhile, then we would either go in to the dance or just hang out all night. We switched back and forth going to Sprite Night one weekend and then Buffalo Bills the following weekend. After a few visits to Buffalo Bills, I met a gorgeous blond girl and four of her friends. We hit it off right away and started meeting at Buffalo Bills every weekend. The girls had friends in Omaha and Bellevue, a suburb of Omaha, and always knew where the parties were.

I didn't let the girls know about any of our drug dealing. But we attended all of the parties we could with the girls in Omaha because the Omaha police didn't harass or break up parties nearly as much as they did in Fremont. Omaha is a much larger town both in population and geographically. Omaha police were busy with an increase in gang activity and an outbreak of home meth labs, and had more important things to do than breaking up parties and handing out MIPs like the police in Fremont did.

During the week, I would stay home and continue to read and watch the media about organized crime. John Gotti of the Gambino family was rising up the ranks quickly. There I was, a teenager, wondering if I would ever be able to put together a group of guys that would stick together to achieve what I had been fantasizing about.

My group of guys started growing up—getting permanent jobs, thinking about college or getting married. They no longer wanted to stay out all night or to be involved in illegal activities; they were thinking about their futures, and *their* futures didn't involve crime.

I guess that's what growing up meant, and to think about my own future, I was confused. What kind of future was that? Going to college and studying for the next four years, then getting an eight to five job doing the same thing day in and day out… then before you know it, there's a wife, kids, and settling into a house. Basically living the same boring life day after day. That's how I looked at it. My way was a lot more exciting. Living on the edge, going out all the time, exploring different places, meeting new people, going wherever or whenever I wanted with a couple grand in my pocket for entertainment.

It wasn't long before a couple of the Omaha girls I had met at Buffalo Bills wanted to come to Fremont and party.

It was a Saturday night and I called the girls to tell them about the party. They were excited about it and agreed to go. I told them I would pick them up Saturday at about 7:00 p.m. and I would bring a friend. At 7:00 sharp, we picked up the girls and drove to Fremont. We decided to drive around the Fremont State Lakes and show the girls Fremont before we went to the party. We arrived at the party around 9:00 p.m.. In less than an hour, the police showed up.

In order to avoid further trouble we didn't say a word as all four of us calmly walked out the door and walked toward the car. One of the officers approached and asked, "You guys been here long?"

I was standing next to my friend Jen with my head down. I didn't want to get recognized by the officer because of all the trouble I was in the year before. Jen smiled and said "It was too crowded so we are going to my house."

The officer said, "Alright, clear the area and be on your way then." As we started walking away, I glanced over my shoulder and saw that the officer continued to walk to the front door. We rushed to the car and got out of there fast and headed back to Omaha.

We went back and hung out at Jen's house for the rest of the night. Jen and the other girl commented on how they had never seen that many police officers before just to break up a party. I told the girls that's how it is in Fremont, the police have nothing better to do or any major crimes to contend with, and that if they had to be an officer in Omaha they might not know what to do.

Prior to this party, it had been quite a while since I had gone to any parties or done any activity in Fremont. About two years to be exact. It was now 1989. I started having smaller scale parties again in Fremont, as well as going to other parties. I met a new group of guys at these gatherings who would stick together for five or six years. One of the guys held most of the parties, so I went ahead and let him. This way I wouldn't have the police over to my place all of the time.

I quickly got back into the life of dealing cocaine and various other kinds of drugs. I had jobs along the way and worked hard at whatever job I had, but they didn't last long. Partying, dealing and trying to become the number one guy in the area at any cost was far too important to me at the time. While I had been out of the game for a couple of years, my reputation in Fremont seemed to have gotten bigger, because I had spent so much time in Omaha.

I started going to the bars and using my brother's identification to get in because we looked so much alike. One of my main hang out bars was one of the local strip clubs. After I had been going to the bar for a while, I got to know the girls and the bouncers pretty well. So well in fact, that the girls would buy *me* drinks, and in the middle of the night if the girls wanted something to eat they would let me use their cars to go out and get food for them. I would go wherever they wanted to buy food and bring it back.

I told a friend about my relationship with the girls and about going to their hotel rooms and partying with them and he started going with me to the bar. After a couple of months, I began dealing cocaine to the girls, which was easy because the bouncers knew. In fact, they were in on the dealing as well.

The bouncers would point out which girls were cool and which ones were not. My friend never used drugs or dealt in them, but he didn't care if I did because he got to party with the girls too.

After the bar closed each night, we would go back to their hotel room. One night, one of the girls asked me if I wanted to do some coke with her. "Sure," I said, "But my friend doesn't use any drugs, so let's go to the restroom and do it. Gotta respect your friends."

When we came out of the restroom my friend Greg wanted to leave right away.

"Why?" I asked him.

"Let's just go," he said.

So we left. On the drive home, I told him that the girl was a road girl, a traveler, and that we both probably would have gotten laid. Greg told me the reason he wanted to leave so quickly was that the girl had left her purse on the bed so he took the liberty of helping himself to some of her money and some of her CDs. He had stolen about $80 and four CDs.

This got my mind thinking and we put a plan together quickly. We started preying on the road girls that came into town and we always made sure we went back to their hotel rooms every Saturday night. I would keep them busy in the restroom with giving them lines of cocaine and Greg would rifle through their stuff.

We would also have small parties on Friday nights. We would charge $2-$5 extra for the booze we would buy for every minor and we sat around and drank along with them.

Greg and I were becoming good friends with the strippers that were called house girls. These are the girls that were there most of the time from Omaha and Lincoln. They trusted us so much that they would have us count their tips in between dance sets. While they were on stage we would count their money but at the same time put some of the tips in our own pockets.

We often ordered rounds of drinks on them. During the length of time that we did this, none of the girls noticed any of their money missing. The girls would just put the money in their purses and at the end of the night leave without counting it. This was a wide open field for two guys with bad intentions. To keep the scam going we never dated any of the house girls because we knew if the relationship ended badly, that girl would talk shit about us to the other girls telling them not to hang out with us, and our diabolical and genius scam would be over.

The attention of the Fremont police was pretty much off of us because I kept my dealing strictly to the strippers. The Saturday night scam was too hard to prove, and if any of the minors that I bought for on Friday nights would ever get caught for MIP, I knew they wouldn't rat on me because I intimidated them and they knew I had a lot of friends.

Eventually I bought alcohol for minors any day of the week. They heard of me through their friends, and knew who I was and how to find me. Most of the time they stuck around and drank with me. Then one fatal Friday night it all changed. A girl had come to my place and asked me to buy her a two-liter bottle of purple passion and a half pint of Everclear. I was having a party that night anyway and needed to go to the liquor store for myself, so I went ahead and bought for her thinking only of the money.

That night, I had my usual set of Friday friends over and partied throughout the night. The next morning a police officer was knocking on my door and asked me to come to the police station. I asked him what for and he replied, "You bought for a minor last night and we need to get your side of the story."

Not really worried about anything, I went along. When I got to the station they told me the girl that I had bought for had rolled her car, and the fire department had to use the jaws of life to get her out of her car. She was in the ICU at the hospital. The first thing they did was take my fingerprints and tried to match them to the bottle they had in evidence. While waiting for this to happen the police were asking me questions trying to get me to admit to buying for her.

I kept my mouth shut until the fingerprint match was completed. The officers told me that there were too many fingerprints on the bottle and they couldn't make a match. They had to let me go once again.

I told a couple of my friends about it that afternoon and they said that they knew her boyfriend. I went to the hospital to see her, snuck in the room where she was, and asked her how she was doing. After we talked for a while, I got up close to her ear and said, "You know, I'm not playing around. I know where your boyfriend lives and it would not be hard for me and a couple of friends to give him a visit, if you get what I mean. It would be best if you no longer pursued these charges on me." She said she wouldn't. As I was leaving, I said "Alright then. Hope you get better."

About a week later the two friends that I had told came to my place and told me they had a talk with her boyfriend. A couple of weeks after that, I got a letter in the mail saying that all charges against me had been dropped. I felt good and bad at the same time; the guilt of her winding up in the hospital was something I would have to deal with for a long time.

LAW OFFICES
SIDNER, SVOBODA, SCHILKE, THOMSEN, HOLTORF & BOGGY

GEORGE E. SVOBODA
NEIL W. SCHILKE
THOMAS B. THOMSEN
BRADLEY D. HOLTORF
S. NICHOLAS BOGGY
BRADLEY E. NICK

MILITARY COLONIAL BUILDING
340 E. MILITARY AVENUE
FREMONT, NEBRASKA 68025

PHONE 402-721-7111
FAX # 1-402-721-9120

S. SIDNER—1875-1944
EARL. J. LEE—1888-1963
H. A. GUNDERSON—1889-1969
ARTHUR C. SIDNER—1900-1975

April 5, 1991

Troy Skinner

Dear Troy:

This letter is to confirm that the County Attorney's office decided not to file a complaint against you on the charge of procuring to minors. Because this matter required less time than anticipated, I have enclosed a check for $75.00. I am withholding the balance of the $150.00 retainer as payment in full for my services.

If you have any questions, please call.

Sincerely,

SIDNER, SVOBODA, SCHILKE,
THOMSEN, HOLTORF & BOGGY

Bradley E. Nick
BEN/cm
Enclosure

This is the letter I received from my attorney informing me that the county attorney would not be pressing charges.

Dodge County Attorney

Dean Skokan

Dodge County Courthouse • 435 North Park Avenue • Fremont, Nebraska 68025
Telephone (402) 727-2725

April 5, 1991

Troy Skinner

██████████████████████

RE: State vs. Troy Skinner, Procuring Alcohol for
Minors

Dear Troy Skinner:

This is to advise you that it will not be necessary for
you to appear in connection with the above-captioned
case on April 16, 1991, inasmuch as the charge is not
being filed.   Thank you for your cooperation in this
matter.

Very truly yours,

Paul Vaughan

DODGE COUNTY ATTORNEY'S OFFICE

bc

*This is the letter from the Dodge County Attorney's office
letting me know charges had not been filed against me.*

CHAPTER SIX

SCAMS ALONG THE WAY

For the next eleven years, I brought together two crews who became involved in more criminal activity than I could even imagine. With the charges of procuring alcohol for a minor being dropped, it gave me an even bigger head so I didn't stop buying for minors. In fact, I started to buy for more so I could make more money.

It wasn't long before I got my first DWI. I had been dating a girl who was seven years older than me. Her name was Lori. One Saturday night I went to one of the popular hangout bars in Fremont. I was drinking at the bar all night and hanging out with friends talking. As the night got later and later I wasn't having any luck picking up any girls, so when the bar closed I got a ride home from a friend.

Once home, I got into my brother's Nissan Sentra which was a five-speed. Not having much practice at driving a stick, I proceeded to go drive to Lori's house. When I got to her house I knocked on the door a couple of times. She finally answered.

"Why are you coming over so late? I'm too tired," she said, and shut the door.

I got back into the Sentra, and headed home. I came to a T-intersection and stopped; I noticed a police car behind me, and another police car on the right side of the intersection—he was stopped, but he did not have a stop sign. I thought, *Shit, I'm going to jail.* I was extremely intoxicated and nervous. I thought I had put the car in first gear and instead I put it in reverse, and backed right up into the police car. *Did that really fucking happen?* I let a few other choice words come out of my mouth as the officer got out of his car and approached my car door. I rolled down my window, stuck out both hands and said, "Cuff me and take me to jail. I'm too drunk to do any sobriety tests and I wouldn't pass them anyway." The officer took me to jail and impounded Rowdy's car.

The next day Rowdy bonded me out. I ended up serving thirty days in jail and losing my license for a year. My mom was upset and heartbroken that I kept getting in trouble with the law, but reluctantly had to deal with the fact that I was getting into that kind of lifestyle. What could she do? She tried to be understanding, but she made it clear to me that she did not condone my actions or behavior.

My mom told me that if I didn't want to listen that I would learn the hard way and that's what I was doing. But I still wasn't worried.

At the same time I started to think about not having a high school diploma and what that might mean later in life. All the people I was hanging out with were three to four years younger than I was, and were receiving their diplomas. I enrolled in a GED class in Omaha and six weeks later, had earned my GED. The year was 1991. I thought I would do something to make my mother happy and proud of me again, even with all the shit I was involved in and all the bad things I had done. I care about my mother a lot so I enrolled in college. My goal was to become a drug and alcohol counselor. I chose that major because I knew both sides. The short and long-term effects and the addictions from seeing it from every angle in my life. All I would need to do is get the counseling side of it down.

School was tough. I discovered that unless my analytical skills were being used for illegal football booking or other gambling activities, math and numbers were never my thing. That would be the eventual downfall of my college efforts. I had earned a 4.0 in my psychology classes, but those math courses would fail me out after the first year.

◆　　◆　　◆

In retrospect, I started thinking that the only thing I was good at was a life of crime. I spent my time continuing to research organized crime, dreaming about how I might be able to put together my scams and dealings into my own organized crew.

The other two legitimate career options I had were professional fishing or hunting, but I didn't have the capital to get started on something like that. For example, I would have had to purchase a $30,000+ bass boat or five or six different guns for the various game in hunting; not to mention the other costs associated with this career. I dreamed of hunting and fishing professionally, and I was good at the sport, but it seemed so far out of reach.

I went back to partying and a life of crime.

◆　　◆　　◆

My brother's underage coworker, Tom, had asked my brother if he would buy some beer for him on a Friday night. My brother agreed, so Tom came over that Friday night and shared a few of his beers with my brother. He then left to go to a high school party. Tom was in school at the Catholic high school in Fremont at the time.

The following weekend my brother had asked Tom if he and some of his friends wanted to come over to have a few drinks. So Tom brought a few friends over with him, Mark, Darin, Dolly, who attended the Catholic school in Fremont with Tom, and Rhonda, who attended the public high school.

They were all sitting around drinking having fun and getting along, and I was in the shower and was unaware that they had come over. After getting dressed, I walked in to the kitchen to get beer and Mark was in the way of the refrigerator, I politely said, "Hey, can you move over for a second?" Then he said, "Who the hell are you?"

I looked up at him. He was about 6'3" and I'm only 5'6", so I grabbed him by the nuts and squeezed real hard and in a stern voice, said, "Move you fucker!"

He moved out of the way and I grabbed my beer, there wasn't much mouth out of him the rest of the night. He and I would become good friends from then on.

The following weekend the same group of people came over again along with some more friends, about six or seven girls and three more guys. I can't remember all of the girls' names but the guys I remember were Joel, John, and Randy.

Tom, Mark, and a couple of the girls would smoke a bowl on my back porch and the smell would drift into the house. I had quit smoking marijuana back in the 80s, but continued using cocaine. I couldn't stand the smell of pot anymore and I didn't want it in the house, so I asked them to not smoke it in or around the house any more. I was involved in enough criminal shit that if the cops came and smelled it, they would have a reason to start searching around the house with probable cause, plus they were all minors.

Rowdy had a few hits of LSD on him, and Tom, Mark, Joel, and I decided to try it. I had heard good and bad things about doing LSD; but being fearless, I tried it anyway. None of us were able to carry on a conversation without laughing, so we told them that we were drinking a lot of Heineken earlier and that we were really drunk.

There were a few girls and guys there that didn't do any drugs outside of alcohol. Out of respect for them, we didn't tell them that we had dropped LSD. From that night on, Joel, Tom, Darin, and I became really good friends, and anytime we would plan on using LSD, we would say we were drinking Heineken as a code.

Rowdy and Mark partying in Fremont.
We had had a few Heinekens.

Before I knew it, the same group of people were coming over every weekend and bringing additional people. Eventually, there were thirteen to fifteen people every weekend, and we all became a close group of friends.

My brother began to see a whole lot of LSD usage, not just among us, but a lot of other people. So he convinced me that we would begin dealing in LSD. Rowdy knew a guy in Lincoln who could get us two hundred hits of LSD for $250, so he called the guy and a week later we drove to Lincoln to pick it up.

The day we drove to Lincoln to get the shit we were extremely nervous, so Rowdy drove, Joel rode along in the passenger seat, and I rode in back with a sauce pan, a can of lighter fluid and a lighter. This was in case after we got pulled over by the cops with the LSD, I was supposed to throw the LSD in the pan, spray the lighter fluid on it and light it, no questions asked.

We saw the financial potential of dealing serious drugs, but were not considering the consequences of getting caught or hurting someone. The penalty was three to five years for every one hit of LSD, and in that first ride, we had two hundred hits. That would have been a life sentence for each one of us. That's some scary shit!

Chapter Seven

TRYING TO BUILD A CREW

This close group of friends of ours was starting to show each other a lot of respect and loyalty. There were times when parties got broken up by the Fremont police, where there were a couple of MIPs given out and nobody ratted on me for buying alcohol for minors.

By this time everybody knew better than to rat because they would get beat by the rest of the crew. The crew had a spoken agreement that if anyone was caught, they were to take their punishment and get it done and over with rather than bringing the rest of the crew down. My brother and I made sure everybody in the crew understood that if they would ever get questioned, especially about MIP violations, it was not something that was going to take down the whole crew. We kept up with the sentencing of certain crimes and the types of searches and interrogations the police would pull, so everybody was ready if any one of us was ever caught. These discussions were part of our regular business meetings.

With this kind of respect and loyalty, the criminal activity started getting bolder. I had met a guy through one of my other friends by the name of Kalvin, he started coming over a lot and proved himself to be loyal real quick. It was my duty to the crew to determine if an individual could be trusted and would be loyal to the group, and I was good at it.

I had heard about a party on a Saturday night and decided to go to it by myself. When I got there and knocked on the door a guy answered and wouldn't let me in. I told him I was coming in anyway because I had previously bought alcohol for most of the girls there. About that time the girl who was having the party came to the door and told me she had enough people in her house. This was a girl who I let party at my house on several occasions, so this really pissed me off. I knew I was outnumbered by the guys there, but I needed to send a message that you don't come to my house and party and think you're going to have a party and not invite me. So I left and drove over to Kalvin's house and told him what had just happened, he became irate and rode back over to the party with me.

This is where he proved himself to be even more loyal. He and I knocked on the door, the same guy answered it, Kalvin right away asked him if he was the one who wouldn't let me in, before the guy could answer Kalvin hit him in the face and he fell to the ground and we walked on in. The girl who was having the party came up to us and before she could say anything Kalvin grabbed her and told her that if she ever pulled any shit like that again he'd throw her through the fucking window. She apologized and we helped ourselves to some of their beer. Nobody else had anything to say. This guy was a real animal, he didn't give a shit about anything. And with the clarity of the message we just delivered, our crew became even more feared. I let him in on what our group was into: dealing of drugs, making money buying for minors, and a few various other things. But we needed more.

Kalvin came up with the idea of stealing tools out of the back of pickups, Mac tool trucks and Snap-on tool trucks, and reselling them on the streets to construction workers. Kalvin had talked to a girl who was in the group to drive the car at night and circle around the block, while we were cutting the locks off toolboxes in the back of pickups. It impressed me that a girl could keep a lid on things because most times they'll tell all their friends, or worse, if they get pinched by the cops, they'll rat.

◆　　　◆　　　◆

While all of this was going on, I decided to join a gym and take up bodybuilding. Kalvin was working out at that gym and he was strong and big. He had talked to me about working out to get more size on me to be stronger in fights and have more power in my hits. Being 5'6", Kalvin told me that if I put more mass on my frame, I would be stronger and essentially, even more of a bad ass.

After a while, I started looking at the bodybuilding magazines laying around the gym, and I began seeing the size of the professional bodybuilders. I imagined myself competing and dreamed what it would be like. It was the first time in my life that I was thinking about something other than committing crimes as my career. I thought about what it would take to become a professional bodybuilder. I read the magazines, asked guys at the gym, and eventually designed a program for myself that would allow me to get there.

I trained hard on the dungeon-type gym equipment for two hours every day. I took mass amounts of protein. I didn't stop drinking or drugs as part of my plan, but my program was working to put mass on my frame. Working out and training came easy for me and I really enjoyed it. I could visualize myself in the magazines and on stage.

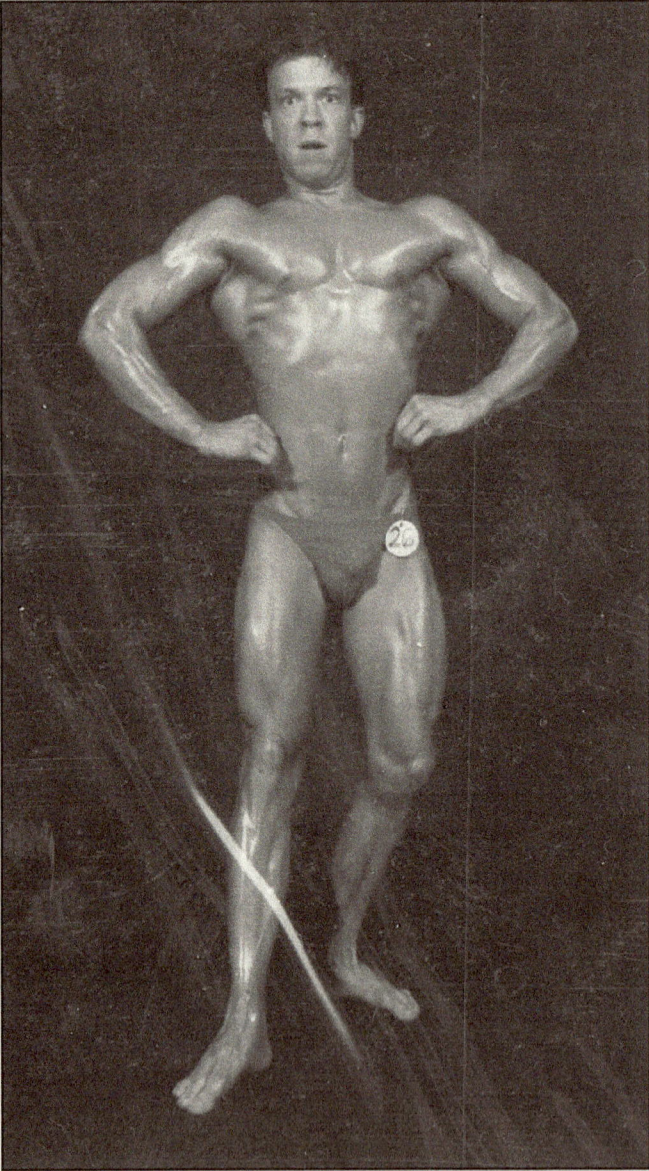

My first bodybuilding show, Omaha, Nebraska, 1994.

Dieting, preparation lead to big finish for Skinner

Fremont bodybuilder finishes second in bantamweight class

BY SCOTT STRENGER
Sports Editor

A little preparation and a little dieting added up to a big finish recently for bodybuilder Troy Skinner.

Skinner, a 25-year-old from Fremont, competed at the 1994 NPC Natural Mid-States Muscle Classic in Rockford, Ill. Skinner said he placed second in the bantamweight division for competitors weighing 143 pounds and under.

"I felt like I did the homework and the dieting I was supposed to," Skinner said. "I felt it (the competition) was judged fairly, but if I would have had a couple extra months to do more homework and more training, I think I could have finished first."

By finishing second at the Nov. 5 event in Illinois, Skinner said he qualified for the Junior Mr. USA meet scheduled for the spring of 1995 in Chicago. The top two placers in each division qualified for that meet.

Skinner said he also was selected to compete in Europe in August of next year as part of Team USA.

In addition to his weightlifting regimen, Skinner said his training for the NPC Classic included a strict diet limited mostly to skinless chicken breasts, fish, non-fat yogurt and water.

"I had to change my diet," Skinner said. "No junk food."

Skinner said his weight dropped to 122 pounds while preparing for the meet.

"The diet was pretty hard to stick with," the 5-foot-5 Skinner said. "I was constantly hungry, but I got through it.

"Now, I'm looking forward to the next two meets and then going pro."

The bodybuilder credited his uncle, Ken Ewald, for motivating him to continue training.

Skinner also credited trainer Allan Mittelstadt for helping him stick to his diet.

"I trained for it (the NPC Classic) for five months," Skinner said, "and in all that time, he only allowed me to have one Big Mac."

Skinner said most of his preparation time for the Junior Mr. USA meet and the Team USA competition will focus on leg work.

See SKINNER, B1

Skinner

From Page B1

"I'm going to have to work out on my legs twice a week, and work twice as hard as I have been," he said.

Skinner said he has plenty of work to do to do before becoming a professional. He said he would like to weigh in at around 165 pounds before trying to turn pro.

"I wouldn't get anywhere being as light as I am," he said. "I'm going to have to pack on size."

Article that appeared in the Fremont Tribune after I finished second in my first show.

Bodybuilder Skinner opens construction on possible career

BY SCOTT STRENGER
Sports Editor

Fremont resident Troy Skinner has just opened construction on what he hopes will become a career as a professional bodybuilder.

Skinner competed in the Heartland Muscle Classic recently at Omaha Burke High School.

The 25-year-old Skinner, participating in his first bodybuilding competition, placed in two divisions in the short class for bodybuilders 5-foot-6 and below.

He finished second in the novice Nebraska men's division and was fourth in the open Nebraska men's division.

"I think it worked out a lot better than I thought it would," Skinner said. "I thought I'd come in last or next to last, but I liked the results so I'll keep on training. I will go somewhere with it."

About 30 contestants took part in men's and women's competitions at the event, Skinner said.

Skinner started working seriously with weights three years ago and competed as a powerlifter. Skinner, who said he has been able to do his training in the Fremont Bergan weight room through the help of Bergan football coach Larry Martin, shifted the emphasis of his training to bodybuilding two years ago.

"I realized I wasn't good enough to make it to the top (in powerlifting)," Skinner said. "I thought I'd have better luck in bodybuilding because you don't have to lift heavy weights to build muscle. It's more reps (repetitions) and form and diet."

Contestants in bodybuilding are scored by judges in three areas, Skinner said. Mandatory poses count for one-third of the score and an optional routine counts for another third of the

See **BUILD**,

A second article appeared a few days later in the Fremont Tribune.

Build

From Page B1

point total. The final third of the scoring is based on the bodybuilder's proportion, or how well each area of the body is developed.

The 5-5, 150-pound Skinner said he plans to continue working toward getting a professional bodybuilder's card and competing in pro events.

One of Skinner's main goals is to compete in the October 1995 Mr. USA tournament, which he said will be televised by the ESPN cable network. Skinner said he hopes to add 25-30 pounds of muscle to his frame by that time.

"I've got to get a lot bigger and eat better," he said. "I'll need to eat a lot of protein."

44

My membership at that gym lasted only a year and a half because, although I became great friends with three of the guys that lifted there, the owner and I didn't get along at all. On top of his attitude toward me and putting me down to all of the other members there about my drug dealing and running a crew, his sister happened to be a probation officer. I had taken his other sister on a date which sent him over the edge and he became vindictive towards me. It was not a pleasant experience so I left. I started lifting at the Bergan Catholic High School gym. Although I took my training and weight lifting seriously, I was still doing what I knew best: drug dealing and running a crew.

Training with NFL defensive tackle, my friend Brad Otis, in Bergan Fremont High School's weight room.

◆   ◆   ◆

One day, my brother cooked up a plan to try and pull an insurance fraud scam to bring the crew a little bit more money. The people involved were myself, Kalvin, Darin, Susan and my brother. Darin had a ski boat and we all went skiing every weekend at the Fremont State Lakes, so this was the setting for the scam. My brother drove a Hyundai that was beginning to have major mechanical problems, so he decided to try to get a big payout of insurance money out of it.

The scam began with Darin, Susan, Rowdy, and I going water skiing on a Saturday afternoon. Darin drove his truck to the Lakes with the boat attached, while Rowdy and I rode together in his car and Susan drove her car to a prearranged meeting place. We were on the lake for about three hours skiing and having a good time. At the end of the day, Darin attached his boat to his truck and drove back to his place. Rowdy and I jumped in Susan's car to ride back into town, leaving Rowdy's car at the Lakes.

Later that night at around midnight, Darin drove back out to the Lakes where Rowdy's car was parked. Darin got out of his car and poured five gallons of gas all over Rowdy's car inside and out. When he was done, he got back in his car and drove about a hundred yards away. From there, Darin walked back towards Rowdy's car, took a book of matches from his pocket, lit one, and flicked it at the car. Darin later told me that when the gas ignited the flames were so big and hot that it knocked him to his knees. He got back up and ran to his car and hauled ass out of there.

The next day the investigation began by the Fremont police, detectives and Fire Marshal, the investigators questioned my brother first by asking him why he left his car at the Lakes, and if he had any major enemies. Rowdy, acting in shock, told them he left his car at the Lakes and rode back with Susan and I to eat and change clothes, planning to go back to the Lakes later that night to do some partying, but we just didn't get back out because we had had a few beers. Then the investigators asked Rowdy if he did it himself. Of course Rowdy said, "No, in fact I'm selling the car to Kalvin." Rowdy told them where Kalvin lived to go ask him about it.

They went over to Kalvin's house and took him to the police station to question him, and when he was being questioned he acted surprised about the whole thing as well. Kalvin told them Rowdy and he had just worked out a deal three days earlier to buy the car. Unsatisfied with Kalvin's statement, they continued questioning him for some time but they released him after a couple of hours of interrogation.

On a Tuesday afternoon a week and a half after the whole thing went down, Rowdy called me from work and told me that the investigators couldn't come up with any hard evidence of arson, so the insurance company is getting ready to cut a check for the car and send it in the mail in the next few days. I replied by saying, "Alright," and hung up the phone.

About ten minutes later there was a knock at my door. I opened it and it was the police, they asked me if I would like to come to the station and answer some questions, I told them "No!" Whatever questions they had to ask me they could ask me right here. The two officers asked me if Rowdy had burned down his own car, I told them "No. Rowdy was gonna sell the car to Kalvin. It must have been some kids that did it."

Then the officers told me I might as well tell them what really happened, because they talked to Rowdy earlier that morning and that he had told them what took place. I replied by saying, "Well that's funny because I just got off the phone with him about ten minutes ago and he didn't say anything like that, so you can take your asses and get the hell out of here now!"

Four days later, Rowdy told me he spoke with the insurance company again, and they told him they were going to send the check in three days. It was over. We had pulled it off, or so we thought. The investigators had one last person to talk to and that was Susan. They had finally decided to go talk to her and ask questions, she agreed to go to the station with them. The investigators threatened her with one to three years imprisonment if she didn't cooperate and tell them what really happened.

Susan gave a seven-page testimony on what actually happened, who masterminded the scam, and who lit the match. All law enforcement officers that were involved were finally satisfied; they contacted the insurance company immediately and denied Rowdy's insurance check. The police went after two of the four of us that were involved—those two were Rowdy and Darin.

Rowdy was facing three to five years imprisonment for insurance fraud, Darin was facing one to three years imprisonment for arson. After Rowdy and Darin hired their attorneys, the prosecuting attorney started talking about plea agreements and what the penalties were going to be. In the end, the judge gave Rowdy three years probation. Part of his probation was no drinking alcoholic beverages, no going into the bars and no drug use. If he broke probation at all, he would end up doing his three to five years in prison.

Darin was sentenced to one year probation and the same stipulations, if he broke his probation he would do his one to three years in prison.

Our crew iced Susan from hanging out with us and forbid anyone in the crew to have anything to do with her. Susan got plenty of threats, but we knew if anything happened to her and she told police that we were behind it, it would have been a good possibility Rowdy and Darin would go to prison for sure. We made sure none of the threats were carried out, but we also made it well known what kind of a rat she was and that she was not invited to any gatherings again. We encouraged everyone in and out of the crew to give her the cold shoulder as well.

This made Tom, Mark, Darin, Joel, Kalvin, Rowdy, and I more quiet on the things we did, and the things we would do, it made the seven of us an even tighter crew, because we had never ratted or given each other up for anything. And that's the way the shit was supposed to be in a crew. If one gets caught, you keep your head down and your mouth shut, and do your time whatever it may be.

We kept our parties a little smaller after all this happened, and our criminal activities a little quieter. This crew of ours was already too big though, and had grown quite a reputation for partying, drugs, and intimidation.

The Fremont police were always watching us, and seemed to be knocking on my door every other weekend when our crew was thinking of new things and having a couple of drinks. They tried their best to get in the door, but I was not stupid; I knew they needed a search warrant and it always pissed the police off when I told them to leave. I would shut the door in their faces and we would all laugh about it. Joel once made a remark that the safest place in Fremont to have a few drinks, talk about criminal activities and think of new scams was my house. At the time it was true, because the police never had enough evidence, information, or any kind of shit on us to get a search warrant served for anything major that was going on.

The Fremont police were not smart enough to sit down the street on any given Friday or Saturday night to observe and stake out the place. They just thought that sooner or later I would be stupid enough to open the door and let them in. That wasn't ever going to happen.

I also started becoming friends and socializing with more respectable people that weren't into crime or criminal activities at all, so that when I had to face judges and prosecuting attorneys, they could hear and see that I was changing and heading for a more suitable and respectable life. I was continuing to lift weights, and had begun competing in bodybuilding shows.

◆　　◆　　◆

*Me posing by the pool at the 1995
North Carolina competition.*

Fremont bodybuilder competes at contest in North Carolina

BY SCOTT STRENGER
Sports Editor

Fremont's Troy Skinner went muscle-to-muscle with some of the nation's strongest bodybuilders during a recent national meet.

Skinner said he placed seventh out of 11 competitors at the NPC Mr. Junior USA meet May 19-20 at Greensboro, N.C. The Fremont bodybuilder competed in the bantamweight division (under 143¼ pounds) at the event, which served as a national qualifier for those seeking to attain professional cards.

Skinner said he qualified to get a pro card and hopes to do so within the next year.

The performers he went up against from the eastern U.S. were particularly impressive during the meet, Skinner said.

"It was a very tough competition with a lot of extraordinary athletes," Skinner said. "I feel like I need more work because the East Coast athletes were just extraordinary."

Skinner prepared for the event by working out at the Fremont Bergan High School weight room with trainer Allan Mittlestadt and Brad Ottis.

Ottis, a Bergan graduate who now plays on the defensive line for the National Football League's St. Louis Rams, accompanied Skinner on the flight to the event.

"That really helped," Skinner said, "because I'd never flown before."

Flying out to the meet the day before it began had a direct effect

See SKINNER

Skinner
From Page B1

on his performance, Skinner said.

"I came in a little lighter than I wanted to," he said. "They only served little glasses of water on the plane, and I'm used to consuming about a gallon of water a day.

"I lost about six pounds, and I was a little softer than I wanted to be."

The meet was taped by Muscle Sport USA and is scheduled to be televised later this month by cable network ESPN, Skinner said.

SPORTS BRIEFS

Fremonter places at bodybuilding event

OMAHA — Troy Skinner of Fremont recently competed in the Central States Bodybuilding Championship in Omaha.

Skinner placed third in the lightweight division (154 pounds).

Placing third at the Central States competition earned him a spot at a meet scheduled for September of 1996 in Dallas, Skinner said. Skinner said he can qualify for a professional bodybuilder's card by finishing first in his weight class at Dallas.

Fremont Tribune article about my 1995 competition in North Carolina.

*I'm just entering the stage for my presentation
at the 1995 North Carolina competition.*

Group presentation at the North Carolina competition.

◆　　　◆　　　◆

Well some years had passed since I had any parties at Izaak Walton, so I thought I would get a new membership there, and just have small parties with our crew and a few outside friends.

I did some fishing there as well. I liked fishing and it made it look like I was actually using the membership in the right way. I attended membership meetings, dinners, and fundraisers, and I also rented the main lodge a couple of times which had a seventy-five person capacity. This made it legal to have alcohol out there, but of course, not for minors. So I had someone sit at the front of the door carding people. That way if any members wanted to come out to check, there were no questions asked. On the surface, it looked like I was doing it the legal way; but at the same time I had given a list of people who were allowed in to my front door person, even though they were minors, because I knew and trusted them. It worked out great, other members thought I was respectable and playing by the rules, but I was playing them instead.

One summer Saturday evening our crew decided to go out to Izaak Walton and have a few drinks and laughs. Rowdy bought an eight-gallon keg and we headed out. The cabins were first come, first served. We got there and nobody was using the cabin that we wanted, but there was a family of three camping in their tent about 50 to 60 yards away. We all decided to keep the music down real low, and not get loud or wild and it would be alright.

We tapped the keg, and Joel had brought a small lunch cooler with a bottle of Rumplemintz on ice. We all had just filled up our first glasses of beer.

I had invited Jenny from Bellevue, Neb., to come along to the party. Right away, we went for a walk while Mark walked back up to lock the front gate because he had forgotten to lock it. I said "Remember, the rules of this place state that all members should keep that gate locked to keep the general public out of the area." I told him at least one of the people we were still waiting on would be smart enough to hop the gate and come get the key to let the rest of them in. On his way to the gate, he walked past two sheriffs that were already at the open gate and the sheriffs had asked him about the party and what was going on.

Mark was reluctant to answer them at first until they told him they weren't going to arrest anybody, they just wanted to find out if someone had a proper membership. Mark believed them and walked with them back to the cabin. As soon as they got in the cabin they said, "You're all under arrest for MIP!" They knew our crew wasn't but 20 years old. Why Mark believed them I don't know, police are famous for saying one thing and doing another. Joel remarked, "What the hell were you thinking Mark? You let them in? 'The party is this way boys—come on in!'"

Jenny and I were standing behind a couple of trees watching all of this take place. I told her Rowdy was the only one in the cabin of age and that he was on probation for insurance fraud. I said, "I can't let him go down for this; if he does, he goes to prison." So I told her to walk back into town to my place, and see if she could get a ride back to Bellevue. I went up to the cabin to tell the police I was the one who bought the keg.

When I got to the cabin and told the sheriffs I bought the keg, they arrested me, and let Rowdy go and still gave everybody MIP citations.

The only thing I had on my mind was *how did they get here so quickly and how did they know about us being out here*? Well, that was soon answered when the sheriffs were walking me to their squad car. The man with the family of three that was camping some yards away from us had walked up to the officer all cocky, and said "I'm the one who called you guys from my cell phone."

I looked at him and said, "You fucking rat, it's just a few friends having a few drinks not causing any problems, thanks a lot!"

Rowdy quickly went to the man's car so he could remember his license plate number. He would be dealt with later.

The membership board was not all that upset with me. For some reason or other they seemed to understand this time when I told them what happened. It must have been that I was acting respectable and attending membership meetings and donating money to Izaak Walton League. It also got me a lighter sentence when I faced the judge this time on eight counts of buying alcohol for minors. The prosecuting attorney of Fremont tried to make me look bad

This is the ticket I was issued for "Contributing to the Delinquency of a Minor" at Izaak Walton.

in court by reading off all eight counts of MIP and having each minor stand up. Then when he was done with all of them, he had me stand up, and said, "Your honor, this is the man who provided all the alcohol to all of the minors, and his name is Mr. Troy Skinner." And then my brother's probation officer stood up and said to the judge, "Your honor, we don't recommend probation, we recommend jail time because on several occasions I have gone to Mr. Skinner's place of residence and have witnessed minors drinking." I told my attorney, "That's a fucking outright lie, if she did come over and witness that, why didn't she write out any MIP tickets?"

My attorney quickly stood up and told the judge what I had just said. The judge had to believe him because there should have been MIP tickets given out. So by her not telling the truth to the judge and a letter from the board of Izaak Walton more or less stating they weren't that upset about the whole thing, I only got forty-five days in jail, instead of the six months my attorney told me I was going to get a day earlier after he spoke with the judge.

I did my time. However, I used that time in jail to continue working out on their universal gym—not ideal for bodybuilder training, but it was better than sitting on my ass waiting for the minutes to endlessly tick by.

◆   ◆   ◆

I got out of jail on a Monday at 8:00 a.m. and went directly home to relax. It was nice to sit in a decent chair and lay in my own bed. I hung around the house, enjoying my freedom and the peace and quiet.

The liquor store that I frequently used to buy booze for our crew was only three blocks from my house. Saturday evening came and I went into the store to buy a bottle of wine. The owner asked me, "Hey, you watch football?" I said, "Yeah, Dallas Cowboys is my favorite team." He leaned over the counter and asked, "You interested in a bookie sheet?" I had known him for years, so I said "Sure!" He gave me a sheet, I glanced at it quickly, folded it up and stuck it in my pocket and left.

Later that night, some of the guys came over to the house and I let them look at the sheet. Rowdy, Darin, Tom and Joel gave me the bets they wanted to place, and I took them back up to the owner of the store the next day. No money changed hands, just their bets written down on a piece of paper.

Over the weekend, we watched all the games at my house. There were eight or nine games that the guys had bet on going on all at once. My entertainment came from watching the guys flip back and forth through the TV channels trying to keep track of their bets. Every guy lost that night—except one—the bookie.

I collected the money from the guys and paid the bookie. So naturally, I got to thinking about a couple of us becoming our own bookies; there was minimal risk of getting busted. I would pick up a new sheet every Wednesday, take bets and I'd be collecting money by the following Wednesday and paying out on Thursdays. I spoke with Rowdy and Darin about my plan. I would make copies and give them to Tom to hand out at Midland College, because he was attending Midland by that time.

We would give the owner of the liquor store a $20 bet once a week so he would keep giving me bookie sheets. If we got too big of a bet from someone we didn't think we could handle we would just hand it off to the owner of the liquor store.

This turned out to be really profitable really quick. We had a lot of guys from Midland betting with us, and before I knew it a few guys from Wayne State college, two restaurants in Omaha, as well as a police officer and a judge's son, which provided a layer of protection.

We were placing about two hundred bets a week, making a few thousand dollars a weekend, and if a bet got too one sided, we devised a plan. For example, if we had everybody betting on the Dallas Cowboys and they were playing the Cardinals, I told people, "I can't take any more bets on the Cowboys." People would start betting on the Cardinals so we could even out the 10 percent bookie fee. This way if there was $1000 on the Cowboys and $1000 on the Cardinals we didn't care who won or lost because we still made our $100 from the 10 percent fee. Our betters didn't care; they just wanted to bet. Some people bitched, but we would tell them to go fuck themselves and go place bets with someone else then, and they always came back to us sooner or later. Now that's good customer service.

I ran the books and all three of us placed and took the bets. We were soon buying the most expensive brands of alcohol and taking our friends out to eat all the time. Darin made a statement once while we were eating, "Isn't this great, dining on the loins of organized crime?" We all laughed and said, "Here, here" and toasted our glasses.

If there was a scam to be carried out, our crew was on top of it. If there was money to be made, our crew was in on it.

The football booking seemed a little more respectable to me than dealing drugs, and a lot less risky. We didn't think to save any money. We were spending it as fast as we made it, but we were living the life weekend after weekend. Until we took four big bets one weekend and we couldn't pay out the big bucks they had won. But then again, we thought wrongly, *what were they going to do—muscle it out of us? People didn't muscle us, we muscled them.* However, if someone was a day or two late on paying us we went knocking on their door; we got our money one way or another.

The four people we owed started telling other people that if they won big, we just wouldn't pay them, and there was nothing they could do about it. This was true, and people started not betting so much or they just stopped betting altogether. We fucked that one up ourselves. Those people were our friends' friends, and were just a faceless number on a page and we didn't care if we fucked them over back then.

CHAPTER EIGHT

I WAS TWO DIFFERENT PEOPLE FROM DAY TO NIGHT

I had slowed down on dealing drugs and reduced my criminal activities. I overheard the owner of one of the local Fremont pharmacies, who just happened to also own all of the Sav-N-Sams Fireworks, talking one day about how he needed to find people willing to sell fireworks at his stands throughout Iowa, Kansas, South Dakota, Colorado, and Nebraska.

Immediately thinking of how to turn this into a scam with big-dollar potential, I told him I would be interested. The owner told me I would have to go to Alliance, Neb., for ten days and sell the fireworks. He would send all the fireworks out in a U-Haul and have them dropped off. He told me that I would make $1000 or 10 percent of what I sold whatever would be greater. He also informed me of my independence and that there wouldn't be anybody coming around to check inventory or pick up money because it was so far away.

I took a friend along with me by the name of James. We arrived a day early. We got to the fireworks stand that was already there and the fireworks were inside, all we had to do is unlock it, and begin to set up for sales.

James and I discussed where we were going to sleep. I said, "Well we can stay at the hotel for $40 a night," so that's what we agreed on. We quickly set up the stand and started selling a day early. We sold $200 worth of fireworks, until the Fire Marshal came late that afternoon and told us we were a day early on selling. We both played stupid and said we were sorry, but our boss told us to start selling. The Marshal believed our story and told us not to sell any more until the next day. We called the owner the next morning and told him that it rained the night before and some of the fireworks got wet while we were trying to set up. He believed us and said, "Try and not let any more get damaged!" So we split the $200.

For the next ten days of legal selling, the scam was to raise our prices by two cents per small item, and more for larger items (as long as they were still cheaper than the other stands' merchandise). The owner of Sav-N-Sams had the other fireworks stands in Alliance beat by four cents per item, so we still had everybody beat by two cents per item when it comes to people buying fireworks, they will shop around for that little bit of price difference.

To keep track of our cut while not leaving too much of a paper trail, we would just make a slash mark on a piece of paper for each kind of item we sold. At the end of the day we would take our marks, add them up accordingly, and pocket the money. The owner never lost money, the customers were still happy and buying fireworks because we were still cheaper than other stands in town, and we were making extra money on the side adding up to $60 to $70 a night.

To boost our sales even more, I had my friend that played in the NFL come out to Alliance to hang out in the stand for one day. We told people as they came to buy fireworks who he was and he would sign autographs for kids. Word of this spread quickly throughout the small town, and for the last three days of selling, even though he was no longer there, our average of $60 to $70 extra per night went to $80 to $90 per night.

When James and I got back to Fremont, we went to the owner's accountant to turn in the profits and she wrote us a check for $1,300. I gave James his half and with the extra money we made every night off the scam, we each had made between $1400 to $1500 apiece.

A day later, the Fire Marshal contacted the owner of the Sav-N-Sams to let him know that we had opened the stand a day early and that their license had been revoked for Alliance for five years. Needless to say, the owner was not happy with us and we stayed away from him. I never set foot in his stores again.

Rams player #95 is the friend that helped me draw a crowd at the fireworks stand in Alliance, Nebraska.

◆　　◆　　◆

My brother had moved to Omaha to take a bartending position at a TGI Fridays. I visited him in Omaha and saw firsthand how much potential there was for larger-scale activities, and I already knew the Omaha police didn't bother people as much as the Fremont police did. Also the corrupt police, the judges and prosecuting attorneys in Fremont always seemed to convict a person based on their past, and what kind of person they were rather than what they were on trial for. In addition, if a defendant hired an attorney from outside of Fremont, it seemed to bring on a stiffer sentence.

I continued to enter bodybuilding shows, usually placing first or second. I still had hopes of becoming a professional bodybuilder, and I saw those dreams beginning to materialize. I started to see things change in myself and in the crew, and my days in Fremont were numbered anyway.

I evaluated the corruption in Fremont and knew there would be no way to continue what I was up to. Our crew slowed down significantly on getting together on weekends, pulling scams and dealing drugs. A couple of the crew members had moved into Omaha. I decided it was time for me to move to Omaha, too.

I had just won the 1996 Mr. Nebraska Bodybuilding Show in my division as a lightweight. My friend Adam was getting out of the Army after eight years of service, and he also wanted to move into Omaha.

Adam called me from Fort Riley, Kansas, where he was stationed and told me he was getting his honorable discharge in November and to find an apartment for us. I had only searched for about two days and found an apartment complex off of 114th and Davenport Street. I called Adam back and told him about the apartment, that it was a great location.

Five minutes from the Westroads Mall, close to eating places, World gym was five minutes away and there was a nine-foot deep pool in the complex. It sounded good to him, so I went ahead and put the deposit down on the apartment, and within a day, I was a resident of Omaha.

I quickly applied at a place called Strategic Marketing. Having had some telemarketing experience in the past, this was easy work for me. I had my interview with them the next day. The hours were great, they had a laid back work environment, and the people were nice. I took the position of a telemarketer and began the very next day. Adam was trying to get on at the police department. He was a military police officer in the Army, but that didn't really bother me because we had known each other for years and he knew what I was into. He just asked me to not have any activity or traffic at the apartment, and I respected his wishes.

I was beginning to work more and focus more on my bodybuilding rather than be out on the streets. I had met a good group of guys at World Gym where I had gotten a membership. One of the guys' was Alex. He accepted me and trusted me right away, the others in the group didn't trust me all that much at first. Alex and I started becoming good friends. He stood about 6'1" and weighed about 265 pounds and had been lifting weights for about five years.

We went out on a Friday night for a couple of drinks and I asked him how he got so big, he had replied by saying, "I eat enormous amounts of protein, use steroids and train hard." I told him I had been thinking about using steroids for a while, but I couldn't find anybody that had any. He told me if I was serious about using them to bring $70 along with me and show up at his place the next day around 2:00 p.m. I left it at that and hung out the rest of the night with him talking about bodybuilding, nutrition, and life in general. I was intrigued by his intelligence; he was not just some dumb weight lifter, and neither was I.

CHAPTER NINE

THE BEST MOVE I MADE

———————

The next day, Saturday, I went to Alex's place at 2:00 p.m. like he had told me to. When I got there I told him I had the $70. He went to his bedroom and came back with two bottles of injectable steroids and handed them to me and said, "Keep this to yourself."

I said, "Which bottle would be best for me to put on size?" He pointed to one of the bottles. "This one, the T-200." I asked him how much the other bottle would cost me, and he told me $60. I had another $100 in my pocket so I bought both bottles and asked him how many cc's a week I should take. He handed me ten new one-inch needles and three-cc syringes. He told me how much of each to take.

Never having used needles before, I asked him, "Hey, what's the best injection site?" He said, "Either your shoulder or your ass cheek."

I went back to my place. First thing Monday morning I took the bottles out of the medicine cabinet, and drew up one cc of T-2, thus beginning my steroid use. I made sure

I ate a lot of protein throughout the day and trained hard. About a week and a half later, I noticed my muscles were a lot fuller and harder, and my strength was increasing. By the end of my first eight-week steroid cycle, I had gained sixteen pounds, my muscles were bigger and harder and looked better than before. Seeing how easy it was to put this much size on in a little amount of time led me into a few years of steroid use. At the time, nobody shared with me, nor did I know, about any of the bad side effects I would experience later.

All of the guys at the gym were a lot bigger than me and my goal was to become a pro in the sport of bodybuilding. Hanging out with these guys kept my ambitions alive, but I realized I wasn't going to make it as a pro because the statistics show that only one percent of all athletes ever make it pro. Even so, I gave it a good run for a few years showing up in different bodybuilding shows across the US, appearing on Fox Sports Network's *Muscle Mania*, and in a couple different magazines.

Getting into the sport of bodybuilding helped me to give up my cocaine use. Alex, the guys from the gym, and I continued to go out and we stayed a real close group of friends. I started dealing steroids, and within a year of living in Omaha I was introduced to the drug GHB. I liked this drug, because it only lasted three to four hours and it also released growth hormones in my body, so it was helpful in bodybuilding as well.

During the week I would continue to make it a point to meet more respectable people and become friends with more business type people. I tried to limit my criminal life on the streets to just weekends. Alex and I would go out on weekends to use the drug GHB at bars and sell quantities of it mostly to other guys who lifted weights. I was becoming more and more impressed with GHB because while I was under the influence of it I could talk to any of the girls in the bar without caring about being rejected.

Alex was always careful not to give anyone too much because for one person it would be fine, and the next it could be fatal or cause a black out. A person on GHB can become really stupid, not making any sense or acting crazy within thirty minutes. I never worried about that because Alex was always with me to make sure that didn't happen to me. That is, until one Saturday night when the guys from the gym decided to go out to one of the popular dance bars in Omaha, and they invited me. I showed up at the bar around 10:00 p.m. and the guys were already there. I saw them standing off in the distance so I walked over to them. "Crazy Kevin" handed me a bottle of GHB, I took an enormous swallow of it and gave the rest back to him and talked to everyone in the group for about ten minutes. I went up to the bar and ordered a vodka tonic.

On the way back to the group, the GHB started hitting me really hard and everything started getting really blurry and I couldn't put one foot in front of the other. That's the last thing I remember. Three hours later I woke up in the hospital with an IV in my left hand, a catheter in me, an oxygen mask over my face and a heart monitor hooked up to me.

I asked the nurse what had happened to me, and she began to explain that I had passed out at the bar, went into convulsions, urinated myself and was brought to the emergency room by an ambulance. When I arrived, I flat lined for nine seconds and the doctors used the crash cart to bring me back to life. She also told me that there was a girl out in the hallway claiming to be my girlfriend and that she was the one who called the ambulance. There were two police officers in the hallway waiting to talk to me as well. Not having a girlfriend at the time, I wanted to see who called the ambulance and who had such a concern for my life, so I told the nurse to let her in the room.

It was Tracy, a friend of my brother. I had only met her twice through Rowdy, she told me she called Rowdy at TGI Fridays and told him what had happened. At about that time, the two officers came in the room and started asking me a bunch of questions like, what I had taken, who gave it to me and what kind of drugs I was on. I was doing my best to avoid their questions by asking them questions back. It worked to buy me a little time.

Rowdy arrived at the hospital a few minutes later, and when he got to my room he told the two police officers that they could not question me in my current condition or under the influence of a drug overdose. The two officers knew Rowdy was right and left the hospital.

I cheated death that night, but I continued to go out on weekends with Alex and the group from the gym. Rowdy continued his big night life, but I was surprising myself by dreaming of buying a house and wanting to settle down. I couldn't quite let go after being in this type of life for my entire life. It was hard, because let's face it, at some point in everybody's life most people would like to be well known for something. I had that, I had the loyalty and protection from my friends, the reputation, both good and bad, my name was known and I felt like somebody. So I just continued on with my lifestyle of doing what I could do best, running scams, dealing and making money the easy way.

I was still working at Strategic Marketing and Rowdy had started a window-cleaning company. I closely watched Rowdy get more and more window cleaning clients. I saw the potential of this company making a lot of money and asked Rowdy if I could buy in for half of the business. He agreed, only charging me $200, because he needed to get liability insurance for the company. We made a handshake agreement, I paid him $200, and that was that.

I worked telemarketing during the week and did window jobs all day Saturday and Sunday. I quickly started helping Rowdy solicit the businesses in town as much as I could. By the end of July, we had enough after-construction cleanup of the windows, residential places, and commercial businesses to do, that I quit my job at Strategic Marketing and went to doing windows full time. This was creating enough income for me that I quit dealing and doing any type of criminal activities altogether. It felt like the first step toward settling down, for me at least; and it didn't feel like a boring eight to five job that I had avoided by whole life.

CHAPTER TEN

No More Working For Someone Else

I strived to reach prosperity and wealth with the window cleaning company, trying to always get new clients and thinking of inexpensive ways to advertise. It felt good.

Hanks Bar and Grill in Waterloo, Neb., had been a window cleaning client of ours for about a year. In May of 2000, the owner put the bar up for sale or lease. Rowdy and I contacted the owner and told him we were interested in leasing the bar, but with our police records we could not get a liquor license.

We contacted my old roommate and friend Adam, and asked him if he would like to be partners with us. With his military police background, he would be able to obtain a liquor license with no problem. Adam was excited to do so, and we set up a meeting with the owner, his attorney, Rowdy, Adam and his controlling girlfriend, and myself, on a Sunday afternoon at the bar to go over all the paperwork, how much revenue the bar had made the last year and inventory. After only about an hour and a half of discussion, I handed the owner $5,000 cash for the first and last month's rent, with inventory of food and liquor included. I didn't charge Adam any money for coming in and being a partner because he put the liquor license in his name. My brother and I were silent partners in the bar, but I put up all the money.

On my brother's birthday June 6th, we started the new ownership and took over the bar. All three of us decided to not change the name or any prices and to leave it the way it was because of the existing name recognition in the small town seventeen miles outside of Omaha—even though I really wanted to change the name to Good Fellas.

We all started very strong and putting in equal amounts of hours, Rowdy would work nights, so he could continue to do windows during the daytime so we wouldn't lose any window cleaning clients. I wanted to run all the books from the bar because I had done the books for the window company, but Adam thought he could do the books better than I could because he had a higher level of education than me. Not wanting any confrontations with a life-long friend, I let him.

The bar already had an established clientele, all we had to do is keep running it the way it was. Two weeks after we took over, Adam and his girlfriend went to Chicago for two days. He got back and put his hours in at the bar, at the end of the month he did the books and paid all the bills, there was no profit left over to divide up between the three of us. I didn't think anything of it, because we had to pay for this, pay for that, money for this, money for that, every time we turned around it seemed like we had to have a new license for something, so I let him take care of the books for July.

Right before the end of July, Adam and his girlfriend went to Seattle for five days, he got back and paid the bills, once again no profit to split up. Now I started thinking about the situation a little bit. *Could the scammer have been scammed?* *No*, I thought, *not by a life long friend.*

The next big event was a town get-together called "Waterloo Days." Adam and his girlfriend went to New York for five days while I ran the bar during Waterloo Days. It was the end of August and I had paid all the bills and had $1,900 left over to split between us. My concerns were now raising my eyebrows.

I confronted Adam about it and told him I was taking over the books. This sparked an enormous argument between Adam, his girlfriend, and myself, so I made the decision that I was going to find someone to buy my half and get out of the bar.

A couple of weeks later, on a Wednesday night, I was working the bar by myself. It was around 10:00 p.m. and only one person was in the bar who was drinking whiskey and 7-Up. He was one of the regulars, and his name was Jeff. He noticed I was preoccupied and he asked me if I wanted to get away from my bar and have a drink somewhere else. I agreed, and locked up at 10:30 p.m.. It was a warm summer night and he knew I owned a Mustang convertible, so he asked me to drive.

As we got into my car, I put the top down and we headed for Fremont to have a drink in a new bar that had opened in town, called Fred-n-Oley's. We arrived at about 11:00 p.m., had a few drinks and talked to a few different girls. Jeff asked me if I wanted to make last call at the strip club on the way out of town. I replied, "If we're going to do that, we better leave now because it's already 12:30."

So we stormed out of the bar, jumped into my car, and headed on the way out of town to the strip club. About a mile away from the club, I passed a state patrol car. I was going 40 mph in a 35 mph zone. I continued driving to the strip club and pulled into the parking lot. Jeff and I got out of the car and proceeded to put the top up. As we were doing so, the patrol officer pulled up in front of us got out of his car and asked to see my driver's license, registration and proof of insurance, so I grabbed the stuff he asked for out of the glove box of my car and handed it to him, he told me to have a seat in his patrol car. Right away he wanted to give me a breath test, and I took the test with no arguments, blowing a breath alcohol concentration of .151, the legal limit in the state of Nebraska for drinking and driving at the time was .10. He then asked me to step out of his patrol car and proceeded to give me some field sobriety tests. I failed a couple of them and once again, I was taken to the Fremont Dodge County Jail and booked in for a third offense DWI.

The next morning I woke up in the holding cell, I asked one of the guards what my bail was, and the guard told me $500. Having $600 on me, I told the guard I would bond myself out. He said, "That's fine. All we have to do is give you another breath test to make sure you're sober enough to drive and then you're free to go."

I was taken out of my cell and I blew into another BAC machine. This time I was 0.0 and bonded myself out of jail. Then I had to get my car out of the police impound lot, costing me another $75. I got into my car and headed back to Omaha. On the way, I stopped off at my bar to grab a sandwich. Adam was there working, as I was eating my sandwich, he came to my table and asked me if I would be interested in selling my half of the bar to his girlfriend's brother.

I told Adam I would sell it for the initial $5,000 I put up for it because I had just got a third offense DWI in Fremont and was thinking about moving to Tampa, Florida, rather than going back to face my sentencing. I knew the prosecuting attorney in Fremont was a stickler for upholding the third-offense DWI sentencing, which was a year in jail and a fifteen-year loss of license. No ifs, ands, or buts.

Four days later, Adam's girlfriend's brother called me and asked me to come to the bar. When I got there, he had a $5,000 check waiting for me.

I was now out of the bar, and heading to Florida to see a friend, Dan. I had not seen Dan for a couple of years. I knew he owned his own business, a mail order list company, and was wanting good telemarketers to work for him. Little did I know, avoiding my third offense DWI sentence would change my life forever. All hell was about to break loose, and the next five months would be the beginning of the end.

◆ ◆ ◆

I had put $4,000 and my Mustang as a down payment on a 1999 Dodge Ram 4x4 super V8 magnum truck, because the Fremont police now knew what I drove and I was nervous that they would contact the Omaha police and let them know I had a warrant out for my arrest. I wanted to be a little harder to find until I got out of Nebraska. Two weeks later, I booked an airline ticket to Florida to see if I would like living there.

On the day I left my brother dropped me off at the airport, which was a Thursday morning. I was supposed to return on Saturday night.

After the first night in Florida I called the airline and rescheduled my return flight for Tuesday morning. Dan, his fiancé, and I were having an outstanding time, and they were showing me all around the Tampa Bay area, which included Saint Petersburg, Clearwater Beach, and Ybor City.

Saturday night Dan took me over to his friend's house in Pinellas Park, Florida, and introduced me to his friend, Fred, who in turn introduced me to a guy named Craig.

Fred and Craig took me on a tour of the area during my visit. They pointed out one of the top mobster's houses in St. Pete to entice me with their lifestyle and to further convince me to do business with them.

Fred, Craig, Dan and I were sitting at the kitchen table after Fred had given me a tour of his house which had a nine-foot deep pool in the back yard surrounded by a dozen hot girls in bikinis, new track lighting throughout, new ceiling fans, three bedrooms, an intercom system throughout, two bathrooms, a sunken living room, and a privacy fence around the entire yard.

Fred asked me if I had ever tried ecstasy. The girls in the back yard were overly friendly and seemed to be having a good time. He informed me that they were all on ecstasy. Then Fred and Craig asked me if there was a market in Omaha to sell ecstasy. I told them that I heard the going price was between $25 and $30 a pill. Both of them immediately became ecstatic asking, "Are you fucking joking? Because they said the going price here in Florida is between $11 and $13 a pill."

Fred asked me if I thought I could sell a great number of pills in Omaha. I told him I didn't know the ecstasy dealers or users at all, but I could call Rowdy and he would know. Fred told me to make the call and find out, so I called Rowdy and asked him if he thought he could sell a lot of ecstasy if it was provided. Rowdy asked me what the price per pill was, and I told him around $11. He said go ahead and bring some back, and I left it at that and hung up the phone.

I told Fred that we could sell some, so he put 200 pills in a sandwich bag for me. A couple of hours later, Dan and I went back to Dan's place. When we got inside Dan asked me if he could look at the pills, so I gave them to him. He took 30 pills out of the baggie and said, "This is my fee for introducing

Between deals, we did some four-wheeling in the backwoods in Florida.

you to Fred and Craig. Everybody has to pay their dues along the way." In this life everybody has their hand out for the taking, and those who choose to play in it have to choose their battles carefully.

— CHAPTER ELEVEN —

THE BEGINNING OF THE END

———

Sunday and Monday, Dan and I spent time on the beaches, going out to eat and seeing more of Florida. Tuesday morning came and it was time for me to leave, I was nervous because I had to tape the baggie of pills to the inside of my thigh and get them through the airport and back to Omaha.

Dan drove me to the Tampa International Airport. We made small talk to keep my mind preoccupied so I wasn't so nervous when I approached the security checkpoint. It was pre-9/11, so there weren't any dogs and they didn't pat me down, I just walked through the metal detector and everything went fine. Dan hung out with me at the gate until I boarded the plane.

On the flight back to Omaha, I was thinking of Fred and Craig and how they could live in such nice homes and have wads of hundred dollar bills in their pockets. I would learn later just how big of drug dealers and how big their crew was.

Dan is on the left and I'm on the right, in St. Pete, in 1998. Dan introduced me to Fred and Craig. He passed away in a motorcycle accident a few years ago.

When Rowdy picked me up from the airport when I arrived in Omaha, my nerves calmed down. I was off the plane and on solid ground and no more pills taped to the inside of my thigh. On the drive back to my place Rowdy told me he made some calls and would probably be able to get rid of all the pills by the end of the week.

When Rowdy and I first started selling the ecstasy, I told him we would never sell to any teenagers and he agreed. By the end of the week, Saturday night to be exact, Rowdy and I had sold of all the pills.

The following Monday I called Dan and told him that I would be coming back to Florida in three weeks, because Rowdy and I had gotten rid of one hundred and seventy pills in four days. So once again, I called the airlines and booked tickets to fly back to Florida in the beginning of October.

Friday morning at 7:30 a.m., the day had come for me to fly back, and Rowdy dropped me off at the airport. I got on the plane and was in the air by 8:00 a.m.. I was scheduled to return to Omaha Monday afternoon. I arrived at the Tampa International Airport by 12:30 p.m. on a smooth flight. Dan was waiting there to pick me up. Omaha temperatures were already starting to drop in the 50s and 60s, while Tampa, Florida, was still in the 80s.

Dan and I drove back to his office and I hung out there with him until 5:00 p.m. when he closed the office for the day. After Dan locked up the office we drove to the Sea Breeze grill, an eating establishment on the beach. The table had a great view of the ocean.

While ordering king crab legs and shrimp, Dan told me that he would be taking me over to see Fred and Craig. After eating dinner the waiter brought our bills to us and Dan insisted that he would pay. After arguing back and forth a couple of times, the waiter grabbed Dan's money and walked away from us; we laughed a little bit about it and left.

I knew we were on our way over to see Fred, and when we arrived Fred welcomed us in, and I gave him his $2,200 for the pills.

Fred, Craig, Dan and I sat down in the living room on the sofa, Fred started discussing how Rowdy and I had sold one hundred and seventy pills so quickly and how much we had charged for them, I told them $25 a pill. Then Fred and Craig asked me how many pills I would need this time. I told them another two hundred pills, Fred then pulled out a bag of pills from the coffee table drawer in front of us and counted out two hundred pills, put them in a baggie and handed them to me. If I had to guess I would say there was 1,500 to 2,000 pills in that bag Fred pulled out.

Me in Florida, circa 1999.

Fred and Craig told me they were interested in coming to Omaha and looking at what kind of opportunities were available, and I knew they weren't talking about jobs. This worked out better for me because I was nervous about flying back with the drugs and didn't like flying anyway. I knew Fred and Craig were talking about moving major amounts of drugs, so I told them that would work and Rowdy and I would pick them up from the airport every time they flew in. Fred then put a gun to my head and said, "Alright, but don't fuck us over, understand?" I said, "Yes, I understand!" And it was left at that. Then Fred and Craig stood up from the sofa and said, "Now let's go out back and enjoy ourselves."

When I got to the back yard there was techno music playing, three or four girls in the pool and five girls sitting on the deck. To the left of them was a table full of relish trays, vegetable dips, shrimp platters, different kinds of liquor and mixers.

I sat on a chair next to the girls and made small talk the rest of the night. I had my eye on one of the girls, her name was Sicilia, she was Italian and after talking to her for a while I found out she lived next door to Dan. I asked her if she wanted to leave the party go back to her house and relax for the rest of the night. She said, "Sure, I'm tired anyway."

I got up from my chair and told Dan, Fred, and Craig that Sicilia and I were leaving and that I would see Dan in the morning. Dan told me to have fun and we left. For the remainder of the weekend I spent time with Dan during the day and spent time with Sicilia at night.

Before I knew it Monday morning came, and it was time for me to return to Omaha. Dan drove me to the airport, and once again I had pills taped to the inside of my thigh as I walked through the airport terminals. When I arrived in Omaha, Rowdy was waiting there in my truck to pick me up. Rowdy told me we had to make four stops and the pills would all be sold; so I went ahead and made the stops and he was right—the pills were all gone.

I'm in Florida with Fred and Craig.
I was holding $4000 in cash here doing an ecstasy deal.

Two days later Fred and Craig called me from Florida, I told him the pills were all sold already. Overwhelmed with excitement, Fred told me that he and Craig would be coming to Omaha in two weeks, and to pick them up from the airport.

That Thursday finally arrived and Rowdy and I went to the airport to pick Fred and Craig up at 3:30. We waited for them to get off the plane, and the first thing Craig said was, "How in the fuck do you guys live in such cold weather?" He had never seen snow before or felt such cold weather because he had lived in southern Florida all his life.

Craig bitched and I laughed all the way back to my truck.

We got in and drove to a hotel around the 72nd and Dodge Street area.

After checking into the hotel, we went to the room, Fred and Craig unpacked their bags and then Fred put a baggie of five hundred ecstasy pills on the desk. Fred asked Rowdy and me to take him and Craig around to the hot spot bars in town so that he could start setting up business. Rowdy and I were charged $13 a pill this time, but that was fine with us because we still charged $25 a pill.

All four of us went to the bars and started introducing Fred and Craig to people we knew. Rowdy and I first introduced them to Darin, Tom and Mike, then to everybody else we knew.

We went out Friday and Saturday night to the bars and talked to more people. Before I knew it, by late Saturday night all the pills were sold, and Fred and Craig told me they would be coming back again in two weeks.

When Fred and Craig returned to Omaha again they brought six hundred pills with them. Rowdy and I picked them up from the airport, checked into another hotel for the weekend, and went out to the bars. The same thing happened—all the pills were sold almost immediately.

Large amounts of pills were being moved in a short period of time. Things were moving too fast and were already starting conflicts with other dealers in Omaha. Fred and Craig had an "I don't care" attitude, and had mentioned if any of the other dealers gave them too much trouble that their friends were waiting to come to Omaha and set things straight. Rowdy and I had a feeling that these were the number one guys of Fred and Craig's crew.

Fred and Craig wanted to move into Omaha and could get their hands on a lot more drugs from Florida. Rumor had it that they had mob ties back home.

The weekend came to a close, and Fred and Craig were getting ready to go back to Florida. Fred had told me that this time they would be returning to Omaha in two weeks with a larger amount of pills, and also a half-pound of cocaine. Fred also told me he was going to rent an apartment when he returned, and that Craig would be flying back and forth from Florida. I told Fred that I would start looking for an apartment for him while he was gone, so that when he returned all he would have to do is fill out the paperwork.

Friday afternoon two weeks, later Fred and Craig came back. I told Fred I found an apartment and that he could go fill out the paperwork. First thing the next morning, he told me we would go do it Monday morning and that we all would check into another hotel room for the weekend. So that was the plan. We checked into a hotel around the 120th and Dodge Street area and went to the room.

When all four of us got inside the room, Fred pulled out a bag of cocaine that weighed half a pound, and Craig pulled out a baggie of ecstasy that contained 800 pills. This was our biggest load yet, and it was only going to get bigger.

Fred, Craig, and I decided to go eat Chinese while Rowdy stayed behind and made some phone calls. While eating dinner I told Fred and Craig that after this load I'd be putting a down payment on a house, taking the money I was making with the window cleaning company, opening a tanning salon, and leaving the drug and crime business.

They both agreed because they wanted all of it to themselves anyway, Fred handed me $500 and said, "This is for finding me an apartment. Thanks!"

After eating dinner we went back to the hotel room, Rowdy told us that a couple of guys were on their way over to pick up an ounce of cocaine. At about that time there was a knock on the door, it was Ben, the roommate of a guy that

Rowdy and I had known and sold drugs to for about five years. Ben bought thirty five pills from me and left. I then had to take Craig over to a guy's house to drop off twenty more pills.

Driving away from the hotel, Craig and I got off of 120th Street and headed west down Dodge Street. A police car behind me flipped on his overhead lights and a focused spotlight right on my truck. I instantly thought that it was for my arrest warrant in Fremont. My truck was a four wheel drive with a super magnum V8 360-cubic-inch engine. I hit the gas and was going to head for the closest open field I could find. Right then the Omaha police helicopter swooped down on us just a few feet above the truck. I knew that I couldn't outrun the helicopter, so I pulled over and told Craig to put the pills in the open bottle of beer he was drinking this way the pills would dissolve, but instead he threw them behind his seat.

Two uniformed officers and four plain-clothes officers approached the truck with their guns drawn. I knew right then what was happening. Someone had ratted us to the police. Two of the plain-clothes officers took Craig and me out of the truck and stood us to the rear of the vehicle. Officer Ryan asked me if I had any weapons in the vehicle. I said, "Yes a 12-gauge pump shotgun that I use for hunting, because I pheasant hunt a lot. I have a hunting license in the truck!" He then asked me if he could search the vehicle. I told him "No!" He searched the truck anyway. Officer Ryan put Craig and me in handcuffs and let us sit on the tailgate of the truck. He then asked me who else was in the hotel room. I told him I didn't know what he was talking about.

After the officers searched my truck, they found the twenty pills of ecstasy and the shotgun. Officer Ryan put Craig and me into a squad car and took us downtown to the Omaha Police Department. When we got to the department and into an interrogation room, Rowdy and Fred were already in the same room.

The interrogation began. Detectives started asking all four of us questions and the only thing I was interested in was who ratted us out! Fred and Craig started telling the detectives that the drugs were all mine and Rowdy's, and that they just came up from Florida to party with us and some girls. The detective laughed, and said, "Let me get this straight. You want me to believe that you flew all the way from Florida just to party with Rowdy and Troy and some girls in the middle of winter." He looked at his partner and said, "I'm done with these two. Go lock them up."

I couldn't believe what I was hearing, Fred and Craig were trying to put the whole thing on Rowdy and me.

After taking Fred and Craig out of the room, the detectives came back to the interrogation room, and asked Rowdy and I our side of the story. We told them how the whole thing got started and how all four of us were involved, Rowdy and I were then taken to a cell.

For the next four days, Rowdy and I remained together in a cell. On the fifth day, a guard came to our cell and told us that we must have really pissed of the judge with the amount of drugs we got caught with, then he handed us our papers telling us what our charges were and what our bail was.

Rowdy and I had a $1 million bail a piece, Fred and Craig had a $2 million bail a piece. We were being charged with selling ecstasy to two informants, possession with intent to deliver eight hundred hits of ecstasy and possession with intent to deliver one hundred forty four grams of cocaine. Each count held zero to fifty years imprisonment, except the cocaine charge, which held twenty to fifty years imprisonment.

I hired attorneys for both Rowdy and myself. We had a bond reduction sentence fourteen days later and had our bonds reduced to 10 percent of $10,000. Also that day in court, the prosecuting attorney told the judge and explained to him who the two informants were that led the Omaha police in arresting us. Once again I was shocked. The informants were Jason, the guy we had known for five years, and his roommate Ben.

Jason had gotten pulled over for a fourth offense DWI, and the two of them together had a total of thirty pills on them. Never having been interrogated before by the police, this made it easy for the police to scare the hell out of Jason and Ben about going to prison and to rat on Rowdy, Fred, Craig and I. After I bonded Rowdy and myself out of jail our attorneys told us that we had a good chance at being put on probation because this was our first felony case. But it wasn't over for me. Omaha corrections had a hold on me for my arrest warrant out of Fremont, so I needed another $1,000 to get out of my hold. I bonded myself out from Omaha rather than go to Fremont then bond myself out.

Nevertheless, it was time for me to start over. My credit was destroyed because my truck was confiscated, repossessed and sold on the government-seized vehicle auction. All but $1,000 of my money was gone due to bonds and attorney fees. My name would now be heavily scarred due to news stories on channels 3, 6, 7 and the *Omaha World-Herald*, *Fremont Tribune*, and the *USA Today*.

I called all of our window-cleaning clients to see if we had lost all of them. Surprisingly, we had only lost three of them. So we started right back at the window-cleaning company.

It was a long wait for our sentencing date, but before I could take care of my Omaha convictions, I had to go to trial in Fremont on my third offense DWI. My attorney and I plead not guilty at my first appearance in court. My attorney also talked to the prosecuting attorney of Fremont to see if he wanted to plead my third offense down to a second offense and I would take a one year loss of my license and spend sixty days in jail. The prosecuting attorney didn't want to do any pleading, so we went to trial.

◆   ◆   ◆

It was now June of 2001, and time for me to go to trial. My attorney, Chris Lathrop, told the prosecuting attorney of Fremont that we would go to trial all the way. I took my attorney's advice and started going to an outpatient treatment program for alcohol in Omaha before my second trial. The classes lasted five weeks, Monday and Tuesday 11:00 a.m. to 1:00 p.m., and Thursday 11:30 a.m. to 1:30 p.m.. This was just in case we lost the trial. My attorney could tell the judge I took these classes on my own in hopes of getting a lighter jail sentence, but my attorney told me he didn't think we would lose.

On June 5th the first trial began at 8:30 a.m. Twelve jurors were selected out of twenty five. Then my attorney and the prosecuting attorney selected six of the twelve jurors to be the jury that we had to present the evidence to in order to get a not guilty verdict.

Two of the six jurors were the prosecuting attorney's friends, one of them a banker of the prosecuting attorney and the other one, a lady who actually worked in the courthouse. As I watched these jurors being selected, I thought *the deck is stacked against me this time*. It finally occurred to me that I should be worried. I might have to spend a lot of time in jail and even more in prison.

—CHAPTER TWELVE—

GOING TO PRISON OR NOT!

—————

The prosecuting attorney hated my brother and me. He even told my attorney, "Rowdy and Troy have made a name for themselves, and it started here in Fremont. I will do what I can to win this trial and push for the maximum penalty!" And it certainly looked like it had started.

My attorney was going over exhibits with the judge and the prosecuting attorney, coming to the conclusion that Exhibit 14, which stated that it had been my third offense DWI, should not be mentioned or allowed for the jurors to see. The judge granted this motion. It made the prosecuting attorney extremely upset and he showed his emotions in court by slamming his notebook of paper and notes on the table in front of him.

The prosecuting attorney called the first and only significant witness there was to the case. It was the state patrol officer who had arrested me. He asked the officer questions about how I had failed the field sobriety test and breath test, and looked over at the jury every once in a while.

Then my own attorney began asking the patrol officer questions. He asked him more significant questions, starting with, "What was the reason you decided to follow my client?" The patrol officer answered, "He was going 40 mph in a 35 mph zone leaving Fremont."

"My client tells me that you never turned your overhead lights on, and that you just pulled up in front of him in the parking lot of the Lariat Club. Is that true?"

"Yes, that is true."

"And why didn't you put your lights on?"

"Because I lost sight of him when I pulled out of the spot I was clocking radar from."

"And when you pulled up to my client, was he in the car or outside of the car?"

"He was outside of the car putting his convertible top up. That's when I noticed an odor of alcohol coming off of him."

"And did he have a passenger or was he by himself?"

"No, there was a passenger who was helping him clamp his top down."

"When my client first passed you, did you see him actually driving the vehicle?"

"No, it was dark and as he passed me, I was flipping my rear radar on."

"So we don't know who was actually driving the car!" As my attorney yelled and looked at the jury, I saw the jurors shaking their heads in an up and downward motion. I knew at this time that my attorney had it wrapped up, but still more questions would be asked. This patrol officer had made more mistakes than I realized until it came out in court and the prosecuting attorney of Fremont didn't stand a chance.

My attorney asked the officer, "Did you ever ask my client where the keys to his car were or if he was the driver of the car?"

"No, I never asked him, I just assumed his keys were already in his pocket."

"Did you inform my client when you gave him a field sobriety test or breath test that he didn't have to take them if he didn't want to?"

"No, I just began giving him the test, asking him if he understood what the tests were and what they were for."

"So let's make it clear to the jury. You never saw my client driving the car, you never saw him get out of the car, you never asked him if he was the driver of the car, and you didn't ask the passenger if he had been driving the car. Is that correct?"

"Yes, that's correct."

My attorney's final statement to the officer was, "Thank you. You've been most helpful."

At that time, the judge called an hour break for lunch, instructing the jurors not to talk about the case to anyone outside of the courtroom. My attorney and I went to lunch at a sandwich place around the corner from the courthouse. During lunch my attorney told me the officer didn't do his job worth a shit when he arrested me. I was thankful for that.

We were done eating lunch at about 1:00 p.m. and it was time to go back to the courtroom. The prosecuting attorney and my attorney were about to begin closing arguments.

The prosecuting attorney went first and told the jury that they must bring back a guilty verdict, because he firmly believed I was the driver of the car, the car belonged to me, and I was well over the legal limit to drive. "And don't forget, if he wasn't guilty, he wouldn't have jumped bail."

Then my attorney began closing arguments, by recapping everything he asked the patrol officer and telling the jury they must bring back a not guilty verdict, "Because we don't even know if my client was driving the car and neither does the officer."

The jurors went into the deliberation room as my attorney and I left the courtroom to go outside and talk. We talked about my case in Omaha because I was more concerned about that case than this one. After talking for about an hour and a half, the bailiff called us back in to the courtroom. The jurors came out of the deliberation room, filed into the courtroom and took their seats. The bailiff said "All rise." The judge entered the room and sat down. Right away, the judge asked the jurors if they were ready to read the verdict.

The head juror stood up and said, "Yes we are. We the jurors find the defendant guilty as charged on the third offense DWI and guilty as charged on failure to appear."

When I heard the verdict my head dropped. The prosecuting attorney stood up looked at the jurors and said sarcastically, "Thank you." The judge looked at my attorney and asked him if we were ready for sentencing. My attorney asked the judge if we could have a three-week continuance on sentencing and the judge granted our motion.

As my attorney and I were leaving the courthouse, he told me he would call me on Monday and to just relax over the weekend. How could I relax facing the possibility of one year in jail and worse yet, a fifteen-year loss of my driver's license?

Monday morning, my attorney called me and told me that he had a feeling that Exhibit 14 was put in the deliberation room while everybody was at lunch. He contacted all six jurors over the weekend and asked them if they saw Exhibit 14. He also asked them that if they had seen Exhibit 14, would they be willing to sign a written statement stating so. My attorney got two of the jurors to sign the statement, and I was granted a mistrial.

On Tuesday, September 18, 2001, at 8:30 a.m., my attorney and I were back in court facing the prosecuting attorney one more time. Once again, six new jurors were selected out of twenty five possible jurors. After the jury selection, this time including no friends of the prosecuting attorney, the trial began. It was pretty much a rerun of the first trial.

The prosecuting attorney asked the patrol officer the same questions as he did in the trial before, and my attorney asked exactly the same questions as he did before.

The questioning went back and forth lasting until noon. All of us were excused for lunch by the judge, and my attorney and I ate lunch at the same sandwich place as before. Again, we talked about my case in Omaha, jet skiing, and more or less just bullshitting. At about 1:15 p.m., we walked back over to the courthouse, took our seats in the courtroom and waited for the jurors to take their seats. The judge came in and told both attorneys that they could start closing arguments.

After closing arguments, the jury went into the deliberation room. My attorney and I sat in the waiting room of the courthouse for the verdict to be brought back. After about forty five minutes of waiting we were called back into the courtroom.

The judge asked the jury if they were ready to read the verdict, and the head juror stood up and replied, "Your honor, yes we are ready to read the verdict. We the jury find the defendant on the charge of failure to appear: Guilty; and on the charge of third offense DWI: Not guilty."

The prosecuting attorney's head dropped as he put his hands over his forehead. I stood up looked at my attorney, shook his hand and said, "Yes" then looked over his shoulder at the jury and said, "Thank you! Again thank you!" The judge told my attorney he would set up a sentencing date for October 9th at 9:00 a.m.

The maximum penalty I could get for failure to appear

was six months in jail, but I had about three more weeks of freedom before I was to go back to court. I did my best not to think about it. Nevertheless, Thursday, October 9th came and it was time for me to stand in front of the judge, who I had seen several times before. I knew he had heard about me and my brother's bust in Omaha, and I knew he didn't like me. I also knew the prosecuting attorney hated me.

My attorney and I stood in front of the judge. He asked if we were ready to have sentencing imposed. Then my attorney asked the judge to take into consideration that I had to go to court in Omaha on October 25th. The judge looked at me and said, "Ten days in jail on the charge of failure to appear, being released the morning of October 18th, and a $1,000 fine." I was happy and satisfied with the decision of the judge. Ten days is a lot easier to handle than six months.

On the morning of October 18th at 8:30 a.m., I walked out of jail and my mother and aunt drove me back to Omaha. Now I had one week before I would face the judge in Omaha.

Not knowing if Rowdy and I were going to go to jail, prison, or be placed on probation, I decided to go out to a couple of haunted houses the night before court with Chad, Michelle, and Megan.

Chad and I went to Brewsky's, a new sports bar that had opened up on 156th and Q Street, for a few drinks. Michelle arrived after we had about three drinks and the three of us went to pick up Megan. From there, we went to Haunted Hollow and walked through the place scaring the hell out of the girls. We had some laughs, then decided to go back to Brewsky's around 11:00 p.m.. All four of us ordered drinks and started a game of darts. Three pitchers of beer and an hour and a half later, Chad decided we would go back to his place to drink some more and play cards. On the way there, we stopped off to get a case of beer.

After playing cards, drinking the case of beer, and another

twelve pack Chad had in his refrigerator, it was about 5:30 in the morning. I had court that afternoon at 1:00 p.m., so I laid down and fell asleep on Chad's sofa. Megan slept in the Lazy Boy chair, Michelle on the floor, and Chad slept in his bed.

Chad woke up and went to work around 8:00 a.m. I woke up about an hour later feeling nauseous, so I asked Megan if she would go next door to my place and grab me some Tums out of my medicine cabinet. I laid on the sofa for most of the morning until it was time to start getting ready for court.

I got up and went to my place, took a shower and put on dress slacks, a dress shirt, and a tie as I always did when I went to court. As Rowdy and I drove downtown to the courthouse I was extremely nervous, thinking we were going to go to prison. We waited outside the courtroom for our attorneys to show up. In the meantime, an anchorwoman from channel 7 showed up, paused for a minute and looked at both of us as she walked by. She then went into the courtroom and took a seat with her camera man. This was the same woman who was putting a story about ecstasy on the news once a month since my brother and I had gotten busted. At the same time, the *Omaha World-Herald* seemed to have a story about it in the paper once a month as well.

I remember thinking to myself, *How much more is the media going to blow this thing out of proportion.* When our attorneys showed up, they told us to relax and that everything was going to be alright. When Rowdy and I were called up in front of the judge he looked at both of us and began to lecture the hell out of us on the dangers of ecstasy for a few minutes. Then the judge put both of us on intensive supervision probation for nine months, then one year and three months regular probation. He explained that if we got our probation revoked by breaking the law again in any way, we would serve no less than eighteen months to ten years in prison.

We were ordered to go to the probation office

immediately to begin filling out papers. Our charges were dropped—all except the possession with intent to deliver eight hundred hits of ecstasy. Rowdy and I were shocked and relieved to say the least.

As we were walking out of the courtroom, the newswoman asked my brother's attorney if we had anything to say and he told her, "No comments and hopefully we will never be back here again."

When Rowdy and I got to the midtown probation office we met our probation officers and started filling out papers, answering questions, also having our probation orders read to us. My probation officer asked which one of us had been drinking already, Rowdy and I both told him, "Neither one of us, why?"

"Because I can smell the odor of alcohol."

I replied, "I drank last night for a while."

"Well, why don't we give both of you breath tests? Rowdy, you're first."

So Rowdy blew in the machine and registered a 0.0.

"Well it's not coming from you. Troy, you're next."

I blew in the machine, and by this time it was 4:00 in the afternoon and I still registered a 0.02 from the night before. My probation officer was shocked and asked me "Did you have a good time? Because it will be the last time for the next two years.

With getting off as easy as I did and not going to prison for ten plus years I had made a promise to God and my mother not to go back to that kind of life style.

◆   ◆   ◆

In the end, when it's all over, there is nothing but a lot of time wasted. The year is 2013 now, and all that I've done still follows me. I can't hunt with a gun anymore and that's something that I loved to do. I can still hunt with a bow or air rifle, but I still take a chance on a law enforcement officer arresting me for a felon in possession of a deadly weapon. It's up to the officer if he wants to arrest me or not.

In the last thirteen years, I have done a lot of positive things in my life, I have grown my window cleaning company to the largest in the state of Nebraska. I have finally gone to many, many Mötley Crüe concerts, my favorite band of all time. I have loved the group and their music since 1981, but I was too busy dealing drugs, getting high or trying to put some kind of new money-making scam together to take the time to go see them in concert.

I have since met a very hot, caring, beautiful woman who has been clean herself for five years now. Jenny tells me that meeting me has made her want to stay clean and do much better in her life as well. She was born in Los Angeles, California. She moved to Las Vegas, Nevada, in 1998, and then Jenny and her entire family moved to Omaha, Nebraska in 2008. Jenny and I have also been working on launching her own women's panty line. We also started a Mötley Crüe fan club (like the KISS Army), where all the members get together every other month to spend three hours listening to Mötley Crüe music and talking.

Rowdy, Jenny, and me at a Mötley Crüe
concert in Tulsa, Oklahoma, 2012.

Jenny and one of the street performers at a Mötley
Crüe concert in Omaha, Nebraska, 2011.

Jenny and the announcer at the Mötley Crüe concert in Las Vegas, Nevada, 2012.

*The World's Strongest Woman, Becca
Swanson, trained me for approximately
six months in Omaha, Nebraska.*

Becca Swanson, the World's Strongest Woman.

I'm proud of the more productive and positive things I have done with my life instead of wasting and throwing it away on a life of crime. I wouldn't trade what I have in my life now for any of the past drug and criminal life that I lived.

I didn't get caught at things when I should have been caught. When I did get caught, I got off fairly easy. It could have gone the other way—it was just the luck of the draw on many things. There were so many possible outcomes for what I did—the girl that had to be taken out of her car with the jaws of life could have been killed in that accident, and I could have gone to jail or prison for many years for the many crimes I committed. I didn't get to fulfill my dream of becoming a professional body builder when it was most important to me. I didn't finish school. I hurt a lot of people, friends and family along the way.

I can see now that a life of crime wasn't worth all the risks. I care about other people and I see that others have the right to live their lives in a safe community. Abiding by the laws and becoming a part of regular society has allowed me to enjoy my life much more. This past year, I finally made pro in bodybuilding, too.

If you find yourself living a life of crime, just know that it is your choice! You can live the life you've just read about and end up with nothing left, or in jail, prison, or dead.

I hope the choices you make in life are the right ones for you, and the correct ones for society.

*Enjoying a clean life on vacation
in the Bahamas, 2005.*

*On vacation by myself
in the Bahamas, 2005.*

Jenny on the beach at the Fremont State Lakes.
She was enjoying the view, and so was I.

Moving into my new house in 2007. I discovered that I can still have a nice house and a great life while living clean.

*After cleaning up my act, I was also able to
continue my bodybuilding career in 2007.*

SPECIAL THANKS TO...

My Mother and Uncle Kenny for not giving up on me.

My friends Joey Bergmanis and Gary Haynes for staying my friend after all that I did.

My Fiancée JennyTigani for all the ways she motivates me.

My attorney Chris Lathrop for believing in me and not turning his back on me. (Also for taking a lot of my money. LOL.)

Lisa Pelto and the girls at Concierge Marketing Publishing Services for helping with this book.

My brother, Rowdy, for turning his life around.

All other family members for accepting me after what I've put them through.

www.ingramcontent.com/pod-product-compliance
Lightning Source LLC
Chambersburg PA
CBHW031901090426
42741CB00005B/595